HOW TO MAKE
Kitchen Cabinets

American
Woodworker

HOW TO MAKE
Kitchen
Cabinets

BUILD, UPGRADE, AND INSTALL YOUR OWN
with the Experts at American Woodworker

Introductions by Randy Johnson

Editor, American Woodworker Magazine

FOX CHAPEL
PUBLISHING

Published by Fox Chapel Publishing Company, Inc., 1970 Broad St., East Petersburg, PA 17520, 717-560-4703, *www.FoxChapelPublishing.com*.

American Woodworker, ISSN 1074-9152, USPS 738-710, is published bimonthly by Woodworking Media, LLC, 90 Sherman St., Cambridge, MA 02140, *www.AmericanWoodworker.com*.

Library of Congress Control Number: 2010040772
ISBN-13: 978-1-56523-506-9
ISBN-10: 1-56523-506-1

Library of Congress Cataloging-in-Publication Data

How to make kitchen cabinets / American woodworker.
     p. cm.
Includes index.
ISBN 978-1-56523-506-9
1. Kitchen cabinets. 2. Cabinetwork. 3. Kitchens. I. American woodworker.
TT197.5.K57H69 2011
-684.1′6--dc22

                          2010040772

To learn more about the other great books from Fox Chapel Publishing, or to find a retailer near you, call toll-free 800-457-9112 or visit us at *www.FoxChapelPublishing.com*.

Printed in China
First printing: April 2011

Contents

What You Can Learn

Which styles are the best choices for your project (Making Doors and Drawers, page 52, Building Kitchen Cabinets, page 8)

How to make cabinets, drawers, and doors from scratch (Building Kitchen Cabinets, page 8, Making Doors and Drawers, page 52)

How to complete your projects with the right hardware (Hinges and Hardware, page 106)

How to successfully install cabinets and countertops
(Installing Cabinets, page 180, Laminate and Countertops, page 150)

How to work with specific materials (Laminate and Countertops, page 150, Hinges and Hardware, page 106, Building Kitchen Cabinets, page 8)

How to make simple improvements to your existing kitchen (Cabinetmaking Projects, page 198, Installing Cabinets, page 180)

Building Kitchen Cabinets

Kitchen cabinets are high on the wish list for many woodworkers. Whether they're replacing worn-out cabinets or changing their kitchen layout, woodworkers often view kitchen cabinets as furniture projects that highlight their woodworking skills through the use of fine materials and precise joinery. Whatever the reason, if you need new kitchen cabinets, the information in the following section will provide you with plenty of easy-to-follow instructions for building your own cabinets. You'll also pick up tips for simplifying cabinet assembly and techniques for applying both flexible and solid edge banding to make plywood look like solid wood. There's also lots of useful information on building both traditional cabinets with face frames and contemporary frameless cabinets, also known as Euro-style cabinets. Kitchen cabinet sizes are pretty standard, but even when they're not, the basic approach is the same. In fact, you can apply your knowledge of kitchen cabinets to lots of other projects, including bath cabinets, office cabinets, and even cabinets for your shop.

by GEORGE VONDRISKA

Face Frame Cabinets

MASTER THESE TECHNIQUES TO OPEN UP A WORLD OF PROJECTS

I f you can make dadoes, rabbets, and face frames, you can make almost any cabinet. Master this foundation of skills and you'll be ready to launch into complex variations of the simple cabinet shown in this story. Here's how:

Face-frame cabinets are little more than plywood boxes covered by a solid-wood frame. The frame adds strength and rigidity to the box, while covering the ugly plywood edges. In this story I'll take you through the building of a typical freestanding wall cabinet. The concepts and techniques can also be used for kitchen cabinets, bathroom vanities, and bookcases. There's plenty of room for mistakes, and I've made them all over the years. To stay in business, and provide my students with shortcuts to success, I've developed systems for avoiding these kindling-producing errors.

The heart of my system includes avoiding rulers and tape measures whenever possible. Learn to transfer measurements and you'll ensure accurate results. There are lots of ways to build a face-frame cabinet, but here I use a tablesaw, jointer, planer, and screw pocket jig. I think you'll agree, it's a simple system.

Choose Your Material

Cabinet carcases, (Fig. A, page 12), are commonly made from sheet stock like plywood or medium- density fiberboard (MDF). I use plywood almost exclusively because:

- Plywood weighs half as much as MDF. For a one-man show like mine, ease of handling, in both building and installing cabinets, is important.
- When machined, plywood throws less fine dust in the air than MDF.
- Plywood corners and edges don't ding as easily as MDF, so it's more forgiving when I'm handling it.

Home centers generally carry plywood and MDF with oak or birch veneers. More specialized hardwood suppliers sell sheet stock in almost every species of wood.

Now, let's build a cabinet.

Vondriska glues a joined face frame to the plywood box.

Getting Started

The outside edges of sheet stock are called factory edges. Between the lumberyard and your shop, they get pretty beat up. Here's a dandy way to make sure those ugly edges don't make it into your project:

1. Rough cut parts 1-in. larger (in both directions) than your finished parts, using a circular saw or jigsaw.

2. Mark the best face of each piece.

3. Run the factory edge against the rip fence for a first cut, making the piece 1/2-in. larger than its finished size. This is your reference edge. Label all reference edges so you can keep track of them.

4. Run the reference edge against the fence, and cut the piece to final size, removing the factory edge in the process.

Figure A: Exploded View

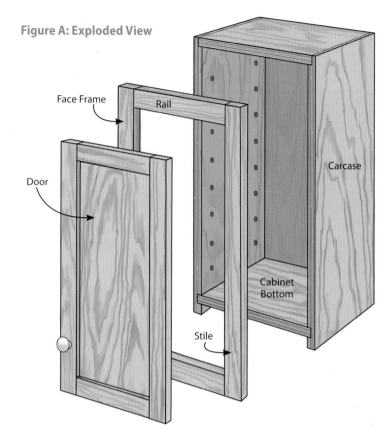

Face Frame

Rail

Carcase

Door

Cabinet Bottom

Stile

X Marks Good Face

Cut plywood parts to width following the four steps above. Feed the pieces smoothly past the blade to get the best-quality cut.

Tip All sheet stock varies in thickness. When possible, cut all the bottoms for multiple cabinets from the same sheet. That way when the dado is right for one piece, it's right for all of them.

Join The Case

2

Crosscut the pieces to length using a tablesaw sled. It's easier to handle large pieces on a sled than on a miter gauge, and your cuts will be more accurate.

3

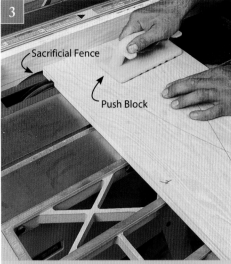

Sacrificial Fence

Push Block

Caution! The blade guard must be removed for all of these dado blade cuts. **Be careful.**

Dado the case sides to receive the cabinet bottom. Be certain the dado head is set up correctly for your sheet stock. The shelf should slip into the dado with no more than hand pressure, and the parts should stick together when you try to separate them. Setting up the dadoes can be fussy, and may require dado shims (thin material that allows you to change the width of the head a few thousandths of an inch). Take the time to get it right. The correct depth for dadoes and rabbets is one-half the thickness of whatever they're being cut into. 3/4-in. plywood gets a 3/8-in. dado.

Tips

- Cut all material with the good face up. Any tearout will be on the bottom, which is the inside of the cabinet.

- For sheet stock, use a 60- to 80-tooth, alternate-top bevel blade for a high-quality edge right off the saw. Don't edge joint plywood or MDF. The glue in these materials is hard on jointer knives.

- Organize your cutting so all same-sized parts are cut together. It's hard to get your rip fence back in exactly the same spot twice.

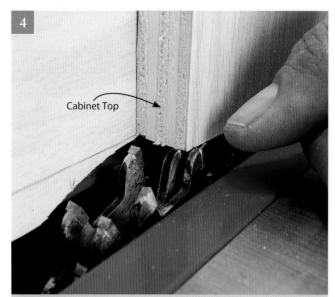

4

Cabinet Top

Caution! The blade guard must be removed for all of these dado blade cuts. **Be careful.**

Position the rip fence for rabbeting. It's almost impossible to get every rabbet perfect, so I intentionally make them 1/32-in. too deep. (Too deep is better than too shallow!) With the saw unplugged, position the fence by using a cabinet top as a gauge. Feel for a fingernail catch where the dado head projects past the face of the top.

Make a test cut in scrap material to check the fence position. There should be a thin leaf of material on the edge of the rabbet. Slice this off with a sharp chisel.

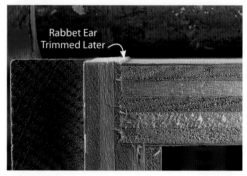

Rabbet Ear Trimmed Later

This will leave "rabbet ears" that can be trimmed off after the cabinet is assembled.

5

Cut the rabbets on the top ends of the case sides using a push block to hold the material down.

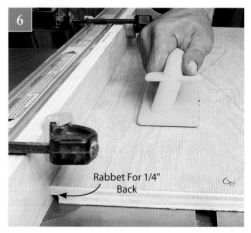

6

Rabbet For 1/4" Back

Rabbet the back edges of the case sides, top and bottom to receive the back. Use the procedure shown in Photo 4 to make the rabbets slightly deeper than the back requires. Don't disassemble the dado head for this thinner material, just bury part of the head in the sacrificial fence.

Making a Sacrificial Fence

A sacrificial fence on the tablesaw prevents you from nicking your rip fence on setups (like for rabbets) that require the fence to be very close to the blade. It's an easily made, must-have tablesaw jig.

You can make a sacrificial fence from any scrap you have, as long as it's flat. (The one shown here is an offcut from my cabinet project.) Here's how to make one:

1. Machine a piece of flat scrap wood to the height and width of your rip fence.
2. Put a 3/4-in.-wide dado head on the saw. Set the head below the surface of the table.
3. Position the rip fence at the right edge of the blade opening in the insert so when you raise the dado head, it won't hit the rip fence.
4. Mark the height you want the scallop to be on the sacrificial fence. I make the scallop 1/16-in. higher than the rabbet I'll be cutting.
5. Clamp the sacrificial fence to the rip fence.
6. Turn on the tablesaw, and raise the dado head until you hit the mark on the fence.

Cut a scallop into the sacrificial fence by raising the spinning dado head to the correct height. If you cut too high, the scallop will be too deep, and the parts you're machining can get caught in it.

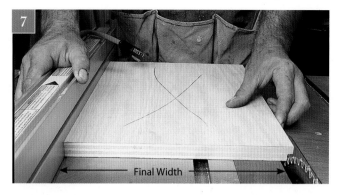

Final Width

Set the fence for ripping the cabinet bottom to its final width. Cutting off the rabbet allows the cabinet back to run full length to the bottom of the case sides. On a wall full of cabinets, I rabbet only one bottom, use it as a gauge, and rip all the bottoms to that dimension.

Stop Collar

Align Here

Brad Point

Drill 1/4-in. holes for an adjustable shelf using a simple jig. Just predrill a hardwood scrap with 1/4-in. holes every 3 in. Mark the bottom end of the jig and line up that end with the dado. Clamp the jig in place, and drill. Two things will give you cleanly drilled holes: a brad-point drill bit (see inset photo), and a slow feed rate as the bit enters the material. A stop collar on the bit prevents unsightly ventilation holes on the outside of the cabinet.

Assemble the Case

Assemble the case, keeping the front edges flush. Clamp pads protect the wood surface. Old plastic honey bottles make great glue bottles—just keep them out of the reach of children. Use just enough glue in the joint to cover the surface; it's just like applying paint.

Glue Brush

Clamp Pad

Check the cabinet for square by measuring from corner to corner. The two dimensions must be the same. If they're not, squeeze the long diagonal by hand, to make it match the short diagonal.

Make the Face Frame

To fit the face frame, throw away your ruler and mark the pieces directly from the case.

Rip the face frame pieces to width with a jointed edge against the fence. Make them 1/16-in. wider than the finished size so the sawn edge can be cleaned up. Use a push stick for these narrow pieces. My rule of thumb for keeping both thumbs is to use a push stick on rips less than 3-in. wide.

Plane the face frame parts to width. Gang planing is an excellent way to make sure all the parts are uniform. Plane the parts until they line up with the bottom of the case sides and the top of the case bottom.

Transfer the stile length directly from the cabinet sides. Make the face frame slightly longer than the cabinet. The rabbet-ear overhang provides the perfect allowance, creating a frame overhang on the top of the case. The excess will be trimmed off after the face frame has been glued on.

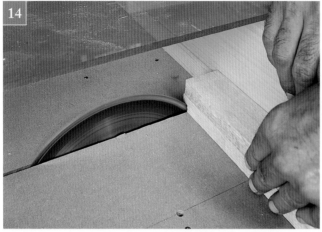

14

Cut the stiles to length using the tablesaw sled. Cutting both stiles at the same time ensures they'll be the same length.

Pocket screws are perfect for face frames—they're fast, strong and easy.

Self-Drilling Tip

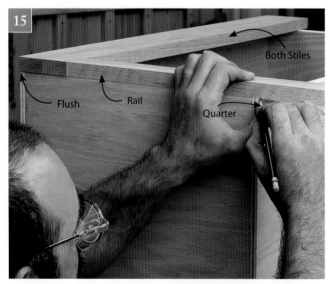

15

Both Stiles

Flush

Rail

Quarter

Transfer the rail length from the cabinet, again building an overhang into the frame. This time use the thickness of a quarter to create the overhang. Start with the two stiles flush with the case side. Butt the squarely cut reference end of a rail to the stiles. Hold a quarter against the case side, and mark the rail flush with the face of the quarter. Cut the rails to length in the crosscut sled.

16

Use screw pockets to join the rails to the stiles. Face frames can be joined by dowels, mortises and tenons, mini-biscuits or simple, fast, effective screw pockets. Mark the rail faces and be sure the holes get drilled only in the backs of the rails. Incorrectly flipping parts around has put some rails in my scrap pile.

17

Rail

Stile

Toggle Clamp

Assemble the face frame in a simple jig. The toggle clamp holds the pieces down firmly. Use a screw designed for screw-pocket joinery (see photo, at left). They don't require predrilling of the stiles, and their wide, flat heads make them less likely than conventional wood screws to split the rail ends.

18

Trim the rabbet ears using a flush-trim router bit (photo below). This guarantees the case sides are even with the top.

Glue Frame to Carcase

Tap a brad into each corner of the case front and snip off the heads. The sharp spur left behind prevents the face frame from slipping and sliding around while you're gluing it on.

Snipped
Brad

Glue and clamp the face frame to the carcase. The frame should be flush with the case bottom, have equal overhangs on the left and right, and an overhang on the top. Use clamp pads, and be careful not to crush the rabbet on the back of the case.

Clamp
Pad

Trim to Fit

Trim the face frame flush with the case using a flush-trim router bit.

Building an overhang into the frame and flush trimming to fit after glue-up guarantees a perfect match between the frame and case.

Shelves and Doors

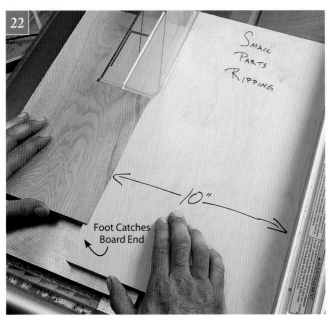

SMALL PARTS RIPPING

10"

Foot Catches Board End

Rip 1/4-in. edging for the plywood shelves using this jig. It lets you leave the guard in place, and safely push the material past the blade. Just set the fence to 10-1/4 in., and allow the foot to carry the material through the saw.

Plywood Edge

Oops!

It's a temptation to cut the face frame exactly the same size as the case. Unfortunately, this often leads to disaster. When you glue the face frame on, it often slips sideways a bit, so you can end up with the unfortunate and unfixable result shown above. The solution is to build the face frame slightly oversize, as we show in Photos 13 and 15.

Hang the door on the cabinet using the hinges of your choice.

Oops!

Sometimes with big cabinets, or if you don't have enough clamps, there may be gaps between the frame and the case. Want a cool fix? Try a flush-trim bit with a V cutter. Line up the point of the V with the seam, flush trim the frame, and the V groove left behind disguises any gaps.

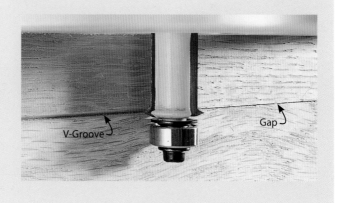

V-Groove

Gap

Extraordinary Flexibility

The techniques in this story can easily be adapted to make many other projects besides classic kitchen cabinets. Here are three examples:

Rolling Shop Cabinet

Make the cabinet out of shop-grade birch plywood, the face frame from birch, and the doors from birch plywood. Locking casters make it mobile.

Bookcase

Add another top, cut curves in the sides and the face-frame rails, and put thicker, wider edging on the shelves. A beading router bit decorated the edge of the face frame.

Bathroom Cabinet

Add some storage in your bathroom with a shallow, wall-hung cabinet. A second plywood top, edged in solid wood with a molding below it, gives the cabinet a more finished look.

This blind dado joint is quick to make and nearly invisible.

by DAVE MUNKITTRICK

Frameless Cabinet Joinery

HASSLE-FREE AND FAST

I've always liked the clean, modern look of cabinets built without face frames. My early attempts involved building plywood boxes first and applying hardwood edging later. But cutting, fitting, gluing, and clamping each edging piece was frustratingly slow—and that was nothing compared to leveling the edging flush with the plywood, a task that was especially aggravating on the inside corners.

I had almost given up making this style of cabinet when I learned a new

Cut all dadoes and rabbets with a router, a pattern bit and a simple dado jig. A couple of offcuts are all you need to perfectly size your dadoes without fussy trial and error set-ups.

technique that streamlines construction. It allows you to put the edging on before assembly. Flushing up the edging on a flat panel is no problem. I can even pre-finish the cabinet parts before gluing them together. I get perfect looking butt joints and an almost invisible line where the edging joins the plywood (see photo far left).

Here's how it works.

1. Cut all your cabinet parts to size. Leave one shelf about 1/2-in. long to use later for test cuts.

2. Cut all the rabbets and dadoes (Photo 1). Because this technique requires consistent dado depth I prefer to use a router and a jig rather than a tablesaw.

3. Glue the hardwood edges to the side panels and shelves by sandwiching a single piece of hardwood between two panels (Photo 2). The hardwood piece is twice as thick as the finish thickness of the edging plus an extra 1/8-in. for the saw kerf. For example, for a 3/16-in. thick hardwood edge

use a 1/2-in. thick piece of hardwood. I like the looks of a thin edge and it still offers plenty of protection for the plywood edge.

4. Rip the glued-together panels (Photo 3). The hardwood edge creates stopped dados and rabbets on the cabinet sides.

5. Flush up the edging with the panels. I start with a block plane (Photo 4) and finish with a light sanding. Using a power sander is asking for a sand-through on the veneer.

6. Trim the edging to length with a handsaw.

7. Use the extra long shelf to set your jointer for notching the plywood (Photo 5). It'll take some trial and error to get the depth of cut just right. The extra length on the shelf allows you to trim and retest the joints' fit.

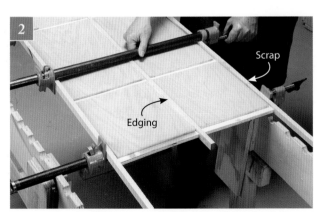

Glue a single strip of hardwood edging to two panels at once. The single piece of edging is twice the desired thickness of the finished edge plus a saw kerf thickness more. Scrap wood protects the plywood edges.

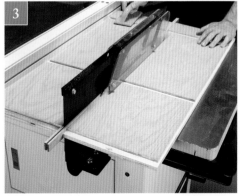

Rip the panels down the middle of the edging.

8. Test the shelf's fit by sliding it forward in the rabbet (Photo 6). If the notched edge butts into the back of the side's edging, the cut needs to be made deeper. If the notch slides over the side's edging and leaves a gap, the jointer needs to be set for a shallower cut.

9. Once you get the right fit, go ahead and notch all the shelves.

10. Dry fit the cabinet to check for any problem areas. An open joint is almost always the result of a high spot in a dado.

11. Do any finish sanding on the edges while the cabinet is clamped together. It's too easy to ruin the fit if you sand the edging when the cabinet is apart.

12. Disassemble the cabinet and finish sand the flat panels taking care not to round the corners on the hardwood edges at the joints.

13. At this point, you can reassemble the cabinet with glue or prefinish the panels and then assemble. Be sure to tape off glue areas and be careful not to build the finish on the shelves so much they no longer fit the dado. I often stain and seal before assembly, then add the last coat or two when the cabinet is glued together.

Plane the edging flush with the panel sides. A block plane gives better control than a power sander. Set the blade for a light cut and ride the plane's heel on the panel.

Test cut a notch on the leading edge of a shelf that's been cut extra long. The jointer's depth of cut must exactly equal the dado's depth. It takes a little trial and error to get the right setting on the jointer.

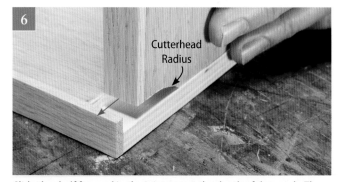

Cutterhead Radius

Slide the shelf forward in the joint to test the depth of the notch. The notch is cut long enough to leave no trace of the cutterhead radius on the hardwood edge.

by BRAD HOLDEN

8 Tips for Building with Face Frames

FACE FRAMES ARE A HALLMARK OF TRADITIONAL CABINETRY, ADDING RIGIDITY AND STRENGTH

Face frames provide a solid-wood surface for attaching hinges and a built-in scribing edge when fit to a finished wall. There are probably as many ways to make face-frame cabinets as there are woodworkers. Here are eight of my favorite tips for building cabinets with face frames.

Plane Face-Frame Parts Together

You'll have many face-frame parts that are the same width. Running them through the planer in a group is quicker than running each piece individually. Hold the pieces together as you feed them, so they stay square to the table. After planing, cut them to their finished lengths.

Use Pocket Screws for Fast Assembly

Pocket-hole joinery is hands-down the fastest way to assemble face frames. Because the holes are on the face frame's back side, they don't show on the finished cabinet. The clamping jig shown here, attached to flat work surface, keeps the parts flush as you drive the screws.

Clipped Brad Nails

Small Brads Keep Frames from Sliding

Glued face frames can slide out of alignment when you apply clamp pressure. If you don't have access to a pocket-hole jig or biscuit joiner, space brad nails every 8 to 10 in. and clip off their heads so that about 1/8 in. remains exposed. Apply glue, align the frame, and clamp it in place.

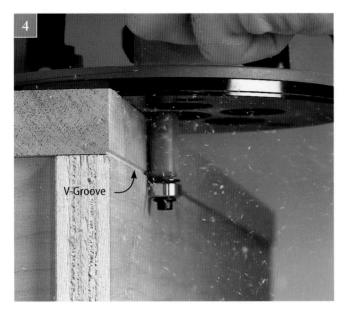

V-Groove

Use a V-Groove Router Bit

The V-groove router bit simultaneously trims the face frames flush and adds a decorative reveal. Start with the face frame about 1/16 in. wider than the case. Line up the V-groove's point on the bit with the joint line where the face frame meets the cabinet and trim the face frame flush. The V-groove visually minimizes the glue line.

Use Biscuits to Align Face Frames

For precise alignment, particularly on long sides, use biscuits. You can use them along the whole frame or just the critical edges. This even works with sides on which you want the face frame to overhang the case. Adjust the depth of the biscuit joiner's fence to accommodate the overhang.

Use Pocket Screws to Attach the Face Frame

Simply glue and clamp the frame in position and drive in the screws. The screws hold the frame in position while the glue dries, so you can remove the clamps immediately and continue working on the cabinet without waiting. Locate pocket holes where they'll be least seen, such as inside drawer openings, on the outside of unfinished ends, or on the inside of finished ends.

Pocket Holes On Unfinished Side

Pocket Holes Inside Cabinet On Finished Side

Overhang the Stile on Finished Ends

This adds a decorative touch and eliminates the step of trimming the face frame flush. I round the face frame's back corner slightly before attaching it to the cabinet. It's easier than doing it after attachment and it gives the face frame a smoother feel and look.

7

Overhang

8

Rabbet On Back of Stile

Rabbet the Scribe Edge

It's rare to find a wall that is perfectly straight, so overhang the stile on the wall side and trim it to fit. Rabbeting the stile's back edge makes scribing easier because you have less material to remove. I like to make the rabbet about 1/2 in. deep, leaving the scribe lip about 1/4 in. thick. Then I use a block plane or belt sander to trim the edge.

by BRAD HOLDEN

Building Cabinets with Pocket-Hole Joinery

NEW TOOLS AND IMPROVED TECHNIQUES MAKE POCKET-SCREW ASSEMBLY FASTER THAN EVER

M any production shops use pocket-hole joinery to build cabinets because it's fast, easy, and efficient. You don't need an armload of pipe clamps. There are no unsightly face-frame nail holes to fill. And you don't have to wait for glue to dry before you move on to the next step.

All these advantages are a boon to the small home shop, too. In addition, pocket-hole joinery doesn't require large, stationary machinery. Everything you need can be stored in a drawer.

Pocket holes are amazingly simple to make. All you need is a drill, a drilling jig and a special stepped drill bit. I'll also share some techniques that make pocket-hole joinery easier than ever.

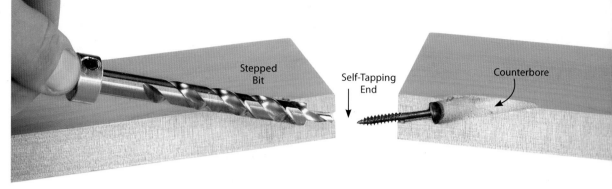

What is a Pocket Hole?

A pocket hole runs at a 15-degree angle. It's created by a stepped drill bit guided by a jig (see Tip 1). The bit's leading end makes a pilot hole; the rest of the bit enlarges the pilot hole to accept the screw's head, forming a counterbore.

Pocket-hole joinery uses specialized screws. They're hardened to prevent the screw from snapping and the head from stripping out. They have self-tapping ends, so you don't have to drill another pilot hole into the mating piece. Screws with fine threads are designed for hardwoods. Screws with coarse threads are designed for softwoods, plywood, particleboard, and MDF. A combination thread is also available for general-purpose use. Pocket screws' heads have a large, flat bottom to help pull the parts together.

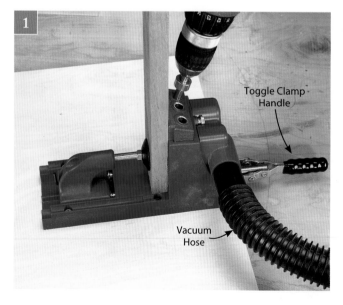

Drill Holes Faster

My favorite new pocket-hole jig has a slick attachment for a vacuum hose. I can just hear you saying, "Who cares about a little drilling dust?" Well, I was skeptical, too, until I tried it. I can drill much faster with the vacuum attached because I don't have to remove the bit to clear chips. In addition, the bit never clogs, and there's no mess to clean up.

Use a Bench Clamp

Here's a way to hold parts perfectly even and flat while you screw them together. It's a locking-jaw clamp that fits into its own special plate. You can surface-mount the plate on a benchtop or a separate board. This device provides that third hand you've always wished for when trying to hold pieces in place and screw them together at the same time. The edges of the plate help you keep the pieces aligned as you screw them together.

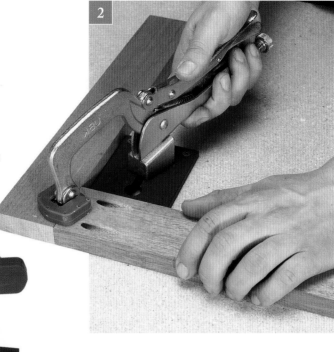

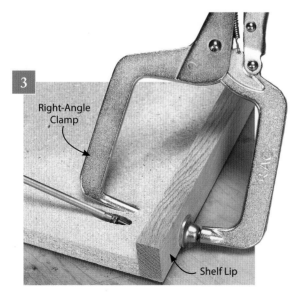

Plate

Clamp Near the Screw

When parts have to fit just so—for example, when you're attaching a hardwood lip to a shelf, as shown here—it's best to clamp as close to the screw as you can. In these situations, I drill two holes side by side. I put a specialized Kreg Right Angle Clamp in one hole and drive the screw in the other. This locking clamp has one round jaw that fits right into a pocket hole.

Right-Angle Clamp

Shelf Lip

Drawer
Front

Assemble Drawers in Minutes

Drawer boxes are quickly and easily assembled using pocket holes. Drill the holes on the front and back pieces of the box. Then cover the holes with an attached front.

Use 1-in.-long pan-head screws for 1/2- to 5/8-in.-thick sides. These short screws have small heads, which dig in an extra 1/16 in. when you drive them. Set the drilling depth 1/16 in. shallower than you would for longer screws.

Assemble an Entire Cabinet

You can use pocket screws when you fasten and glue all the parts of a plywood cabinet, even the top rails. You don't have to fumble with pipe clamps or protect the cabinet's sides from clamp dents. The only trick is to figure out—in advance—where the holes will go so they won't show.

Cabinet
Back

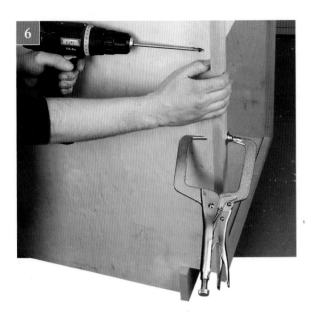

Attach a Face Frame

When you're using clamps, face frames are a pain in the neck to glue on a cabinet—you'll wish you had three arms! Pocket holes make the job a lot easier, because the screws do the clamping. For easier alignment, it sure helps to use a Right Angle Clamp.

Because this side won't show when I install the cabinet, I'm putting the pocket holes on the outside. On a finished side, drill the holes inside the cabinet.

Assemble a Tricky Corner

Slanted corners look great on plywood cabinets, but they are a real bear to assemble. Where do you put the clamps? It's much easier to let pocket screws do the work by drawing the pieces together without clamps.

This method uses a strip of hardwood, rather than just the plywood panels, to form the corner. Using a hardwood strip offers two benefits. First, a solid piece of hardwood is much more durable than plywood veneer. Second, aligning the parts isn't as fussy. You plane, rout, or sand the strip's overhanging point after the joint is assembled (see photo, right). You can't do that with plywood.

To make this joint, rip an angled edge on a hardwood strip. The strip must be at least 1 in. wide for a 135-degree corner. Fasten the strip to panel A with 1-in.-long pocket screws. Drill pocket holes in panel B and assemble the corner. Trim the point flush.

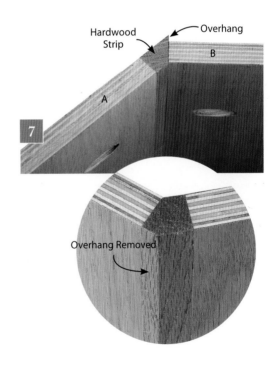

Hardwood Strip

Overhang

B

A

Overhang Removed

Install Bottoms and Shelves

You don't have to fuss with dadoes or rabbets when you use pocket screws to join bottoms and shelves. Drill holes on the underside to keep them out of sight. I use two Right Angle Clamps and drill the outer holes in pairs. During assembly, I work from the outside in. I align the shelf by putting clamps in the innermost side-by-side holes, and then put screws in the other holes.

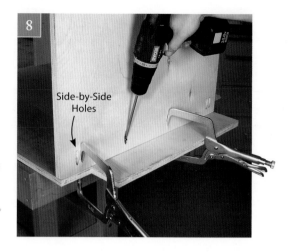

Side-by-Side Holes

Tapered Plug

If You Can't Hide 'Em, Plug 'Em

No doubt about it, a cabinet full of pocket-screw holes doesn't look attractive. If the holes will show, you sure won't want to drill them on the cabinet's outside. They should go inside instead, where you can fill them with plugs. Premade tapered plugs are available in seven different wood species. Glue them in the holes and sand them flush. For melamine cabinets, use plastic plugs. Their caps cover the holes so sanding is unnecessary. You can also use plastic plugs in wood cabinets.

Plastic Plug With Cap

Wooden Plug

by BRUCE KIEFFER

Iron-On Edge Banding

IF YOU CAN IRON A SHIRT, YOU CAN APPLY EDGE BANDING

Iron-on edge banding is a modern cabinetmaker's best friend. It quickly covers the raw edges of veneered sheet stock, saving lots of time compared with traditional glued-on solid wood edging. It takes a finish in the same way as your veneered sheet stock does. Its many uses include covering edges of shelves, doors, and frameless cabinet components. Edge banding is not, however, a substitute for solid wood trim on edges that can get physical damage, such as on a tabletop. Impact from chair backs, for instance, would damage its thin veneer.

Edge banding, or edge tape as it's also known, is simply a veneer of wood, plastic or metal with a coat of hot-melt glue on one side. It's available in a variety of wood species, including birch, cherry, hickory, maple, oak, pine, and walnut. The plastic banding comes in wood grain or solid color for use with plastic laminate and melamine. Metallic banding's many varieties include brass, brushed copper, and aluminum. Edge banding is available in 5/8-in. to 2-in. widths and 8-ft. to 600-ft. lengths. It's pocketbook friendly considering the time you save using it. The per-foot cost depends on brand, species, and size.

You need only a handful of tools to get started with iron-on edge banding. Our recommended starter kit includes a travel clothes iron, a handheld trimmer, and a utility knife. If you've never tried edge banding because you thought it was tricky business, you owe it to yourself to give it a shot.

5 Steps to Apply Edge Banding

Just iron it on. Edge banding is easy to apply. Set the iron on high and use moderate downward pressure. The trick is to move the iron quickly enough to keep the wood from scorching, but slowly enough to melt the glue. It takes a little practice to get it right.

Press the edge banding down with a wood block while the glue is still molten. Rub back and forth for a few seconds until the glue sets. Tip the block along the edges to ensure a tight joint without a visible glue line.

For edge banding longer than 3 ft., heat and press short sections at a time. Otherwise, the glue sets up before you can rub it down.

Tip Cut the edge banding an inch or two longer than the edge you're covering. It makes it easier to position the banding while you iron.

Cut the ends flush with a utility knife after the glue cools. Don't try to cut the tape in one stroke or you'll tear the edge banding. Make several light cuts until the waste piece falls away.

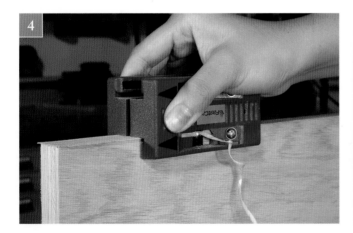

Trim the edges using a double-sided edge trimmer. For under $20, it's the only way to go. The trimmer has two openings with knives that can be set to cut a flush or a bevel edge. We recommend leaving both sides set up for flush trimming, because sandpaper does a better job of easing the edges.

The trimmer is designed for stock between 5/8 in. and 1 in. thick, but you can take it apart and trim one edge at a time on thinner or thicker stock.

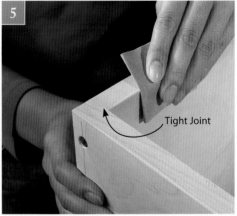

Tight Joint

Ease the banded edges with sandpaper. Edge-band your cabinet parts *before* assembly, but ease the edges *after* assembly. Otherwise you risk having open joints where a horizontal shelf meets the side.

6 Tips for Better Edge Banding

Old Glue

Trim Edges Quickly, Precisely

Cut your end trimming time in half with this tool. It's as accurate as it is fast. It slips over the edge banding's untrimmed edges, rests flush against the end of the panel stock, and easily trims off the excess with a quick press of the handle. It's not inexpensive, but if you do a lot of edge banding, you'll love this tool.

Reapply Heat to Undo Mistakes

One benefit of iron-on edge banding is that it's easy to remove. Just reheat the surface and peel it off. Some of the old glue will be left behind on the plywood edge, but that's OK. Put the new edge-banding piece right on top, and the old glue will blend with the new.

Use Self-Stick Edge Banding on Curves

Self-stick edge banding works great on a tight radius. Iron-on banding tends to pull off the curve before the glue has a chance to cool and set. Self-stick application is easy: Peel off the protective backing, position the edge banding, apply pressure and trim the edges. You're done!

On the downside, though, self-stick is twice as expensive as iron-on banding, it leaves a visible glue line and the sticky trimmings can be annoying. Professionals use self-stick for on-site work where an iron would be impractical. Our recommendation is to use iron-on whenever possible.

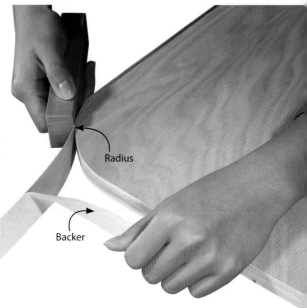

Radius

Backer

Steel Wheel

Roll Faster

This is the Ferrari of rollers. It's used to apply bonding pressure to either iron-on or self-adhesive edge banding. Well-balanced and easy to hold, it has a low profile that's easier to handle with one hand than a J-roller is. The roller speeds the application process because it concentrates pressure at its contact points on both ends.

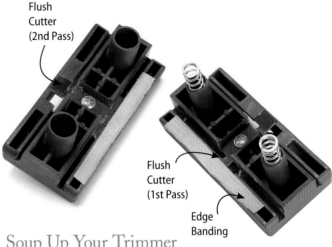

Flush Cutter (2nd Pass)

Flush Cutter (1st Pass)

Edge Banding

Avoid Finger Joints

Real wood edge banding is a series of 6-to 9-ft.-long pieces of veneer connected by finger joints to make full-length rolls. The finger joints can be difficult to see until you apply finish, but then they stick out like sore thumbs. Inspect each strip for finger joints beforehand to avoid putting them on your piece.

Soup Up Your Trimmer

Tear-out can be a problem when you trim wood edge banding. The answer is to modify your trimmer so it leaves a slight overhang after the first pass. Just apply strips of edge banding to the inside edges of one opening in the trimmer. Make your first pass with the shimmed side. This removes most of the overhanging edge. Then flip over the trimmer and make the final cut. Because the second pass is only removing very thin strips, there's little chance for tear-out to occur.

Finger Joint

by DAVE MUNKITTRICK

Tips for Edging

PROPERLY APPLIED EDGING LOOKS GOOD AND PROTECTS FROM DAMAGE

As modern cabinetmakers, we've become so accustomed to using veneered sheet stock it's hard to imagine building cabinets without it. Sheet stock saves time, money and valuable trees.

The veneer can be wood or a man-made material like melamine. The substrate or core for the sheet stock is most often made of MDF, plywood or particle board. The catch to building with sheet stock is covering up and protecting the unattractive and fragile edges. A hardwood strip glued onto the sheet stock edge is typically how this is done. The hardwood edge not only looks good, it protects the edges from damage.

The trick has always been to quickly and efficiently apply the edging and then trim it flush to the ultra thin veneer. What follows is a set of tried and true tips, used by pros, to get the job done.

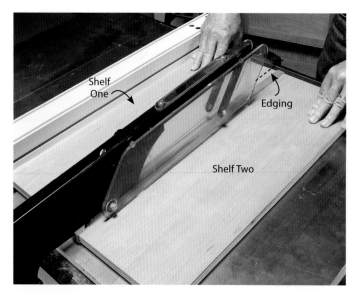

Shelf One

Edging

Shelf Two

Two-for-One Edging

Speed up edging shelves and cabinet parts by gluing them up in pairs. It takes fewer clamps and less setup time. Glue an extra wide strip of hardwood between two pieces of plywood. Don't forget to add the thickness of a saw blade to the hardwood strip. The plywood should be about 1/2-in. oversize in length and width. Glue and clamp the sandwich together. The plywood acts like clamping cauls to apply even pressure along the full length of the joint. After the glue dries, rip it down the middle and trim the ends square and flush.

Easy Edge Clamps

Thin edging doesn't require heavy clamp pressure to get a tight joint. A few pieces of electrician's tape stretched over the edge provide the right amount of clamping pressure and helps center the edging on the sheet stock. It's a quick and easy way to apply thin edging.

Skip the Sander

Plane the edging flush with the veneer. It's quicker than sanding and there's lot less chance of cutting through the thin veneer. Ride the heel of the plane on the veneer and set the blade for a thin shaving, especially when you get close to the veneer surface. Even if you hit the veneer, it rarely cuts through. All that's left is a little finish sanding with some fine grit paper.

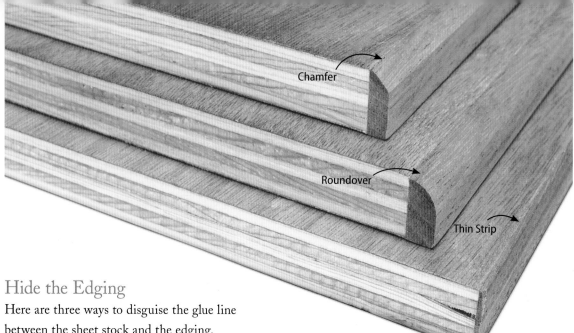

Chamfer

Roundover

Thin Strip

Hide the Edging

Here are three ways to disguise the glue line between the sheet stock and the edging. First, make the edging just thick enough to accommodate a chamfer or roundover router bit profile. Flush the edging to the veneer before routing the profile.

1. For the chamfer cut, set the bit to cut the full thickness of the edge back to the glue line.

2. For the roundover, make the edging slightly thicker than the radius. The curve should begin right next to the glue line.

3. The third method is to glue on the hardwood edging, trim it flush then rip it down to 1/16-in. thickness. A little sanding on all three edging styles is all it takes to blend the transition from veneer to solid wood and obscure the glue line.

Flush Ends Every Time

This well-known tip may seem obvious, but it's worth remembering before you blindly follow any cutting list for edged plywood.

Cut your edging and plywood about 1/2-in. longer than the final length. Glue on the edging and trim both at the same time on the tablesaw. The plywood and edging will be perfectly flush every time.

For edging with an overhang, support the plywood from underneath to get a clean cut on the top surface. The support also minimizes tear-out on the bottom of the plywood.

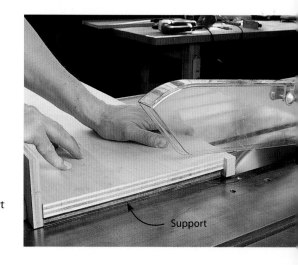

Support

Precision Flush-Trim Jig

Some pieces, like a tall bookcase side, are just too big to trim on a router table. This jig will flush cut edging on any size piece, large or small. You can use any size straight cutting bit, but I recommend a wide mortising bit. The jig is just a 10-in. x 24-in. piece of 3/4-in. plywood with a 1-in. dado cut about 8-in. from one end. Drill a 1/8-in. x 1-in. hole through the middle of the dado for the bit to protrude. Attach the router and add a fence so it just barely overlaps the bit's cutting radius. The bit will ever so slightly cut into the fence.

To set up the jig, lower the router bit until it is flush with the bottom (Photo A). Turn the router on and run the fence along the edging to trim flush (Photo B). The long base on the jig counterbalances the router and the fence guides the cut.

2-Piece Edge Banding Bits

A well-disguised hardwood edge makes a sheet of plywood look like solid stock. Router bits designed to create an almost invisible joint do just that. It's a two part setup. The first bit cuts the deep V-groove in the plywood (Photo A). The second bit cuts the mating profile in the hardwood (Photo B). It's best to work with a wide piece of hardwood. Cut all the V-grooves first.

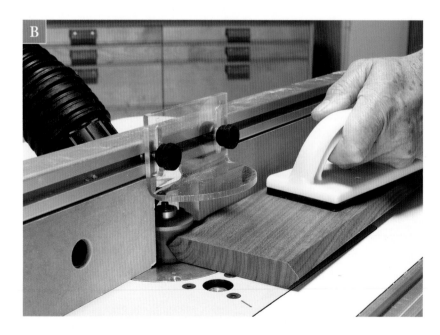

"A well-disguised hardwood edge makes a sheet of plywood look like solid stock."

Then set the bit for the hardwood edge. Cut the matching profile on both edges of the hardwood and glue the shelves and hardwood together (Photo C). After the glue dries, rip the shelves free. The visible part of the hardwood edge should only be about 1/16-in.thick. (Photo D)

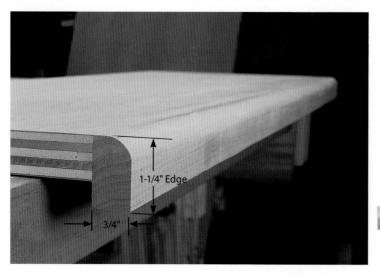

No Sag

Stiffer Shelves

Beef up plywood shelves with wide edging so they can bear more weight without noticeably sagging. I rip the edging from 3/4-in. stock and turn it on its side, giving the illusion that my shelves are made from expensive, thick wood. Nope, they're just plywood!

Flush Cut on a Router Table

Flush up the edging on your sheet stock using a tall fence for support on your router table. The best fence material is melamine because it has a slick surface. Simply screw the melamine to your existing fence. Leave a gap at the bottom tall enough to accommodate the edging. Set the fence so it's flush with the bearing on your flush trim bit. The fence stabilizes the sheet stock as it's held on edge. You can zip through a stack of shelves in no time with this production shop technique.

Use a Flush Trim
V-Groove Bit for Melamine

Edging melamine with hardwood is about as tricky as it gets. To sand, plane or finish the edge without messing up the melamine is next to impossible. Masking off the melamine is a time consuming pain. One way to overcome these problems is to use a flush trim V-groove bit. Simply set the bit so the V-groove is centered on the glue line (Photo A) and rout. Then color the groove with a black Sharpie (Photo B) to create a physical and visual border between the edge and the melamine. The point of a Sharpie fits perfectly in the groove. The slight gap between the melamine and the hardwood edge make sanding and applying finish a snap (Photo C).

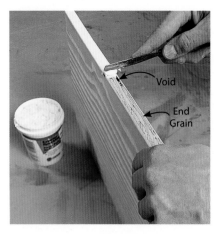 

Void

End Grain

Fill Painted Edges

Make inexpensive plywood look like solid wood by filling voids and end grain with exterior spackling compound. Let the spackling compound dry for half an hour, round over the edges of the plywood with a router bit or sandpaper and sand the edge smooth. Brush on a primer and top coat and you've made economical materials look classy.

Spring Steel

Versatile Edge Clamps

Spring clamps make applying thin edging a snap. Simply squeeze the clamp open, push the flexed piece of spring steel against the edging and let go. The non-marring jaws grip the plywood so the clamp doesn't slide backward. The jaws can be adjusted to exert from 1 to 50 lbs. of pressure.

These handy clamps are perfect for curved edges, where pipe clamps are notoriously difficult to set up.

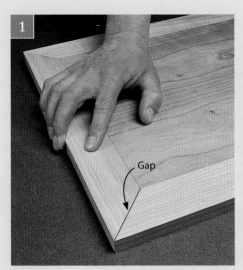

Nuts! There's a noticeable gap between the miters!

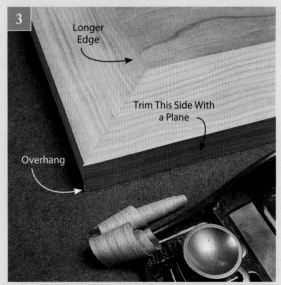

I jointed the inner edge of the mis-cut piece, taking very little off. Because the ends of the board are mitered, the inner edge gets a bit longer with every pass.

Oops!

Wouldn't you know it, I cut the last miter for my framed tabletop too short! Rather than start over with a new piece, I used my jointer to "lengthen" the short piece and make a perfect fit. Sound impossible? Here's one way to stretch a board.

Now it fits perfectly, but the points of the miters don't quite line up because jointing the board made it narrower, too. A little fudging will fix that. I tapered the neighboring frame piece with a plane until the points met.

Making Doors and Drawers

For many woodworkers, building the doors and drawers for cabinets is the best part of a cabinetry project—and for good reasons. More than any other feature, doors and drawers determine the look of the cabinetry. From a technical standpoint, building doors and drawers involves a variety of interesting building techniques, joinery, and tools. It challenges the builder to do his or her very best work for both appearance and durability. Doors and drawers need to be built to withstand daily opening and closing—not to mention the occasional toddler using them as a swing or chin-up bar. Doors can range from simple plywood doors, often referred to as flush doors, to frame and panel doors with flat or raised panels, with styles from traditional to contemporary to creative custom work with inlays, carving, or exotic wood. For the woodworker, drawers are more than just a good place to store stuff. Perfect for mastering the classic dovetail joint, they offer opportunities to learn, practice, and show off joinery prowess.

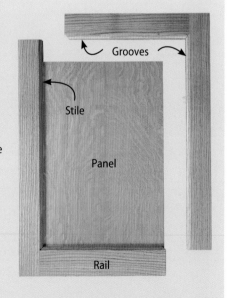

by TIM JOHNSON

Frame and Panel Door

GREAT RESULTS IN 10 SIMPLE STEPS

Name a cabinet's parts, and you're sure to include doors—one of woodworking's elemental structures. Cabinet doors come in every shape and form and they can be made a hundred different ways. This story features a popular form and a foolproof method: Using a router table equipped with stile and rail cutters to create a frame and panel door.

The Door

A frame and panel structure creates a stable solid-wood door (see Door Structure, right). Vertical stiles and horizontal rails form a rigid frame with minimal seasonal movement. The panel floats inside the frame, housed in grooves, so its seasonal movement is hidden, especially if the panel is stained and finished before it's installed.

Usually, the stiles and rails are the same width, but making the bottom rail 1/4-in. to 1/2-in. wider subtly balances the door. Doors look best when the stiles and rails are made from straight-grained stock. This provides an orderly appearance and focuses attention on the panel. Using straight-grained stock also minimizes the door frame's seasonal movement. Panels look best when they're thoughtfully constructed, either to show striking figure or cohesive grain pattens.

Door Structure

A typical cabinet door consists of vertical stiles and horizontal rails that surround a panel. The panel is housed in grooves cut in the stiles and rails. The panel can be flat, as shown here, or have a raised center, with the edges tapered to fit in the grooves. Raised panels are enormously popular, but it's hard to top the understated elegance of a flat panel with pleasing grain or figure.

Grooves

Stile

Panel

Rail

Figure B: The Cutters

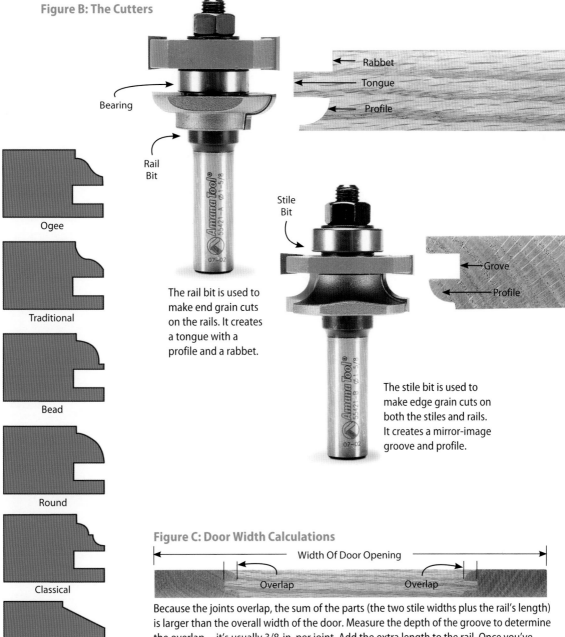

Bearing

Rabbet

Tongue

Profile

Rail
Bit

Stile
Bit

Grove

Profile

The rail bit is used to make end grain cuts on the rails. It creates a tongue with a profile and a rabbet.

The stile bit is used to make edge grain cuts on both the stiles and rails. It creates a mirror-image groove and profile.

Ogee

Traditional

Bead

Round

Classical

Bevel

Figure C: Door Width Calculations

Width Of Door Opening

Overlap

Overlap

Because the joints overlap, the sum of the parts (the two stile widths plus the rail's length) is larger than the overall width of the door. Measure the depth of the groove to determine the overlap—it's usually 3/8-in. per joint. Add the extra length to the rail. Once you've determined the correct part sizes to make the door exactly fit the opening, add an additional 1/8-in. to the width of each stile and rail (Photo 1).

Figure A: Profiles
Stile and Rail Cutters are available in a variety of decorative profiles.

The Cutters

Stile and rail cutters create a decorative version of the tongue and groove joint (Fig. A). They're available as a single reversible bit or in dedicated sets. Reversible bits usually cost less; dedicated sets are more convenient to use. Dedicated sets include separate bits for the end grain and the edge grain (Fig. B). All cuts are made with the face of the workpiece against the table. Reversible bits have to be disassembled and reassembled between cutting operations. Also, some cuts are made with the workpiece face-side-up; others are made face-side-down.

Prepare Your Stock

For inset doors, plan to make your door the same dimensions as the door opening (for lipped and overlay doors, add the lip/overlay widths). Consider the overlapping joints when you calculate the door's width (Figure C). Determining the door's length is easy: Just cut the stiles to the length of the door opening. Door panels are housed on all four sides in the frame's groove, so include the overlaps when you calculate both the panel's width and height.

Include extra test pieces when you rip your stile and rail stock (Photo 1). Once the pieces are cut to length and width, mark their back sides. Use these marks to correctly orient the pieces for routing.

Rip all the stiles and rails 1/8-in. oversize in width. Then cut all the pieces to final length. The extra width allows a second routing pass on the edge grain, if the initial pass causes tearout.

Set the rail bit's height with a test rail installed on the sled. For 3/4-in.-thick stock, position the rabbet cutter to create a 3/16-in.-deep rabbet.

Make the End Grain Cuts First

Begin by routing the rails' end grain. (To remember to rout the rails before the stiles, think of the alphabet: *R* comes before *S*.)

Install the rail bit and make a test cut. (Photos 2 through 4). On the test piece, check the profile's top lip and bottom rabbet. For appearance and strength, the lip should measure at least 1/16-in. and the rabbet should measure at least 3/16-in. For maximum support, don't cut into the jig's backboard during your test cuts. Wait until the bit is set at the correct height.

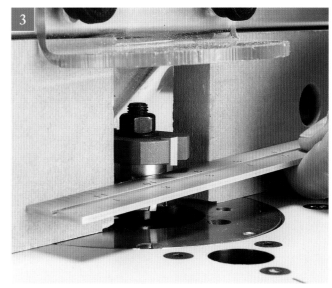

Set the fence flush with the rail bit bearing. This assures a smooth cut, by allowing use of the fence to guide the sled that carries the rails.

Routing Sled for the Rails

Use this sled to make end grain cuts safely and easily. It holds narrow rails squarely and securely and tracks against the router table's fence, which keeps your fingers out of harm's way. It also supports the rails' back edges, to prevent blowout.

3/4" x 5" x 9" Solid Wood Backboard

1/4" x 8" x 9" Hardboard Base

After you've compleed the end grain cuts on the rails, install the stile cutter and rout the inside edges of both the stiles and rails (Photos 5 through 7).

Fit the Flat Panel

With solid-wood flat panels, starting thick and rabbeting is easier than planing the entire panel to exact thickness (Photo 8). If your door frames are 3/4-in.-thick, your panels must be thinner than 7/16-in., so they don't protrude beyond the back of the frame.

Assemble the Door

Before you assemble the door (Photos 9 and 10), sand and finish the panel, including all the edges. Finishing prevents unsightly strips of unfinished wood from appearing in the winter, when the panel shrinks in width, due to seasonal movement. Finishing the panel's edges seals the wood so glue can't soak in and bind the panel to the frame.

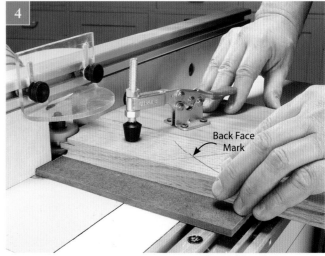

Make a test cut to check your set up. Adjust the bit's height and the fence, if necessary. Then rout the ends of all the rails—your marks on the back faces show when the rails are oriented correctly, face-side down.

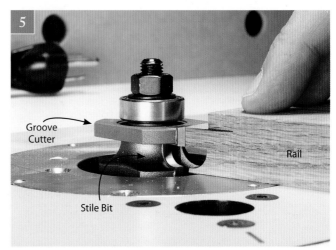

Set the height of the stile bit by aligning its groove cutter with the tongue on one of your rails. Then reset the fence flush with the bearing.

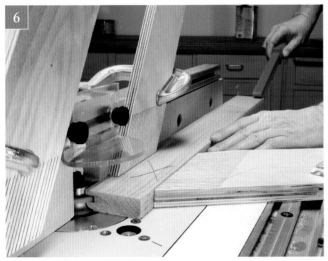

Cut a test piece, using featherboards to hold it in position and a push stick to move it through.

Flush

Check the fit by installing one of the rails. The faces should be flush. Adjust the cutter height, if necessary, then rout all the inside edges. After routing, rip and joint the stiles and rails to final width.

Dealing with Tearout

Tearout can occur when you have to rout against the grain (above). First, thank your lucky stars for ripping the pieces oversize in width. Then rip the stile to remove the tearout (below) and rout again. The lighter cut is less likely to tear out.

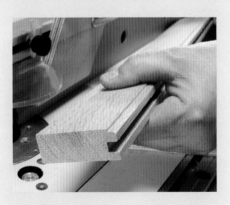

Create 1/4-in.-thick tongues all around the panel to fit the grooves in the stiles and rails.

Fitting Plywood Panels

The bane of using 1/4-in. plywood for door panels, of course, is that it's often less than 1/4-in. thick. That means unsightly gaps or annoying rattling can result when it's installed in 1/4-in.-wide grooves. Here are three ways to cope.

Shims

Solution 1: Wedge the panel from the back to eliminate gaps on the front. Trim the wedges flush to the frame.

Solution 2: Eliminate rattling by installing space balls to stabilize the panel.

Solution 3: Use adjustable stile and rail bits.

Glue the door together one joint at a time. As you go, make sure the outside edges of each joint are flush. First assemble one corner (1). Next, install the panel (2). You should never glue in a solid wood panel, because of seasonal movement, but it's okay to glue in a plywood panel. Position the remaining rail (3) and then install the remaining stile (4).

Assure the door is flat and square. Tighten the clamps gently; stop as soon as the joints squeeze shut. Too much pressure will bow the door—make sure it remains flat on the clamp bars. Measure both diagonals. The door is square if the measurements are identical. You can draw an out-of-square door true by angling the clamps slightly (so they're not quite parallel to the rails) and retightening them. Measure again—if the measurements are farther off than before, simply reinstall the clamps, angled the opposite way.

Tip

Minimize squeeze-out by carefully brushing glue onto the rail ends. Keep glue away from the groove so it doesn't come in contact with the panel.

edited by TOM CASPAR

Slot and Spline Paneled Door

HANDS DOWN, THE EASIEST WAY TO MAKE A FRAME-AND-PANEL DOOR

A good-looking frame-and-panel door is really quite easy to make, if you keep it simple. Just use a plywood panel and a slot-and-spline joint (see photo, below). This door is held together by splines made from 1/4-in. plywood. The panel is 1/4-in. plywood, too. The splines and panel fit into the same size slots in the stiles and rails.

All you need to make the door is a router table and a 1/8-in. slotting cutter (see photo, right). Plywood is usually undersized, so a 1/4-in. cutter would be too big. Instead, you'll make two slightly overlapping passes using the 1/8-in. cutter. That way, you can adjust the slot's width to perfectly fit your plywood, whatever its actual thickness.

Tools and Materials

You'll need a tablesaw, small handsaw, router table, and 1/8-in. slot cutter with a bearing that makes a 3/8-in.-deep slot, though a 1/2-in.-deep slot is OK, too. Slot cutters and bearings are widely available.

A 1/8-in. slotting cutter is the only bit you need to make this door.

Rail

Plywood Spline

Plywood Panel

Stile

If you're making lots of doors, I recommend using an adjustable cutter. You'll only have to make one pass per slot, rather than the two passes shown in Photo 6. Some adjustable cutters use shims, while others can be dialed to various widths. I made my door from 3/4-in.-thick solid wood and 1/4-in. MDF-core plywood, but you can use this technique with any type of plywood or material of any thickness.

Mill the Stiles and Rails

Rip and crosscut the stiles and rails so they have square sides and ends. Note that the rails butt up to the stiles. Make an extra stile or rail for testing the router setup. Mark the stiles and rails (Photo 1).

Rout Slots, First Pass

Install the slot cutter in the router table. To approximately center the slots on 3/4-in. material, raise the cutter 1/4-in. above the table. Exactly centering the slots isn't important. Align the fence so it's flush with the bearing (Photo 2). If your router table is equipped with sliding subfences, push them within 1/16 in. of the cutter. This makes routing end grain safer and more accurate.

Mark the door's parts using the cabinetmaker's triangle. It identifies the top and bottom rails, and the left and right stiles.

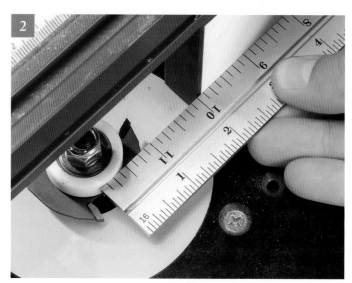

All the joints for this door are cut on the router table. Set up a 1/8-in. slot cutter so its bearing is flush with the fence.

Rout 3/8-in.-deep slots in each stile and rail, face sides down (Photo 3). Rout slots in the end of each rail, face side down (Photo 4). Push the rails with an 8-in.-square backer board.

Rout Slots, Second Pass

Figure out exactly how much wider the slots must be to fit the plywood. Hold a small piece of plywood next to a test piece's slot and mark the plywood's thickness (Photo 5).

Place the test piece on the router table, face side down. Raise the cutter to just below the pencil line. Turn on the router and make a short second pass (Photo 6). Test the plywood's fit in the slot. If you have to use force to push in the plywood, the slot is too narrow. If you can fit two pieces of paper between the spline and the slot's wall, the slot is too wide. When you've got the right fit, make a second pass on all the rails and stiles.

Cut the Spline

Rip a long, narrow strip from the plywood. Cut the strip 1/32 in. narrower than the combined depth of two slots.

Measure the rails to determine the spline's length. The splines run from the outside edge of a rail to the bottom of the slot. Cut the splines to length. The safest way to cut these small pieces is with a bandsaw or with a backsaw and miter box. Put the splines in the rails' ends, without glue, and assemble the door.

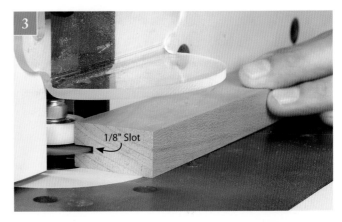

Rout 1/8-in.-thick slots the full length of each stile and rail. Refer to your marks to be sure each face side is down and the inside edge is against the fence.

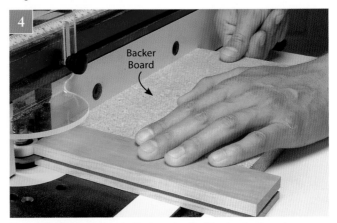

Rout slots in the rails' ends. Push each rail with a backer board. This steadies the rail and prevents tear-out on its back side.

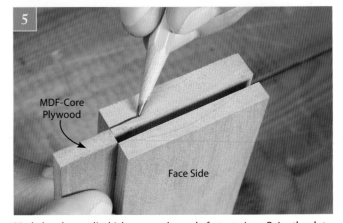

Mark the plywood's thickness on the end of a test piece. Raise the slot cutter to just below the pencil mark.

Cut the Panel

Measure the panel opening. Add 11/16 in. to the opening's length and width and cut the panel to this size.

Glue the Door

Sand the panel and the inside edges of the stiles and rails. Glue the splines into the rail's ends (Photo 7). Put glue on both sides of the splines' slots and on the rails' end grain. Position the splines so they extend 1/32 in. beyond each rail's outside edge. Apply glue to both sides of the splines protruding from the rails.

To make the door as strong as possible, glue the panel, too. You can't do this with a solid-wood panel, because it must be free to expand and contract, but plywood won't move. Run a bead of glue on the back side of the long slots in the stiles and rails.

To assemble the door, insert one rail into a stile. Slide in the panel, then the second rail. Make sure the rails align with the stile's ends. Push the second stile into place and clamp (Photo 8). Sand flush the protruding spline after the glue has dried.

Make a second pass on the test piece to widen the slot. Adjust the slot's width by raising or lowering the cutter until the plywood fits perfectly. Then make a second pass on all the stiles and rails.

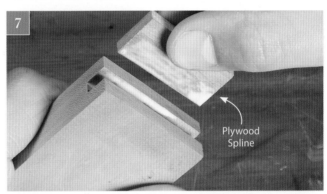

Glue splines into the rails' ends. Apply a bead of glue to the panel slots, too, but only on the slot's back edge, so glue won't leak out the front.

Clamp the door. There's no messy squeeze-out around the panel's front, just in the back. Gluing the panel isn't required, but it makes the door extremely strong.

by TOM CASPAR

Divided-Light Doors

ADD A MASTERFUL TOUCH WITH CLASSIC GLASS DOORS

With the right set of router bits, a divided-light door is a lot easier to make than it looks. The key to success is simple: Measure and cut every single part first. To get you going on the right path, I'll show you a foolproof way to calculate the precise length of every piece. Then you rout, mortise, and assemble. Piece of cake.

Tools You'll Use

To build these doors, you'll need a router table and a set of special bits. You'll also need a metric ruler, tablesaw, planer, jointer, and some means of making mortises.

Design Your Door

Let's start with some old-fashioned terms. The openings for the glass are traditionally called lights. They're "divided" by bars called *muntins*.

Start by drawing your door. Determine the door's overall size, the widths of the stiles, rails and muntins, and the size of the lights.

Anatomy of a Divided-Light Door

Horizontal Muntin

Vertical Muntin

Stile

Mortise

Rail

Tenon

Haunch

Three major parts make a divided light door: stiles, rails, and muntins. Every part is locked in place by a mortise-and-tenon joint. In this six-light door, the two horizontal muntins are the same length as the rails. Three short vertical muntins fit between the rails and horizontal muntins.

Although proportions vary among furniture styles, in this door the lower rail is 1-1/2 times as wide as the top rail. All the lights are the same size and evenly divided.

Next, select a set of divided-light door router bits. Each set is designed for a specific range of door thicknesses and requires a different setup, but the general steps are the same. Visit the manufacturers' Web sites for details. Some bits make tenons; some other sets do not.

Start Cutting Parts

Mill all the door parts to final thickness (7/8 in. for this door). Make a few extra boards the same size as the rails. Use these for making the muntins and for testing the router bit and mortising machine setups. Crosscut all the pieces a few inches long.

Rip and joint the stiles and rails to final width. Cut the stiles to final length. Leave the rails and muntin boards long. The muntins will be 3/4 in. wide, but don't rip them yet. Leave them as part of a wider board.

Two matched router bits cut all the profiles. The cope cutter shapes the ends of all the rails and muntins. It also forms a short tenon and a rabbet to receive the glass. The bead cutter shapes the long edges of the stiles, rails and muntins. It also forms a rabbet.

Both bits may be adjusted to fine-tune the tenon's thickness. You simply take apart the bit and add shims above the bearing. These shims come with the bit and are stored under the nut and washers.

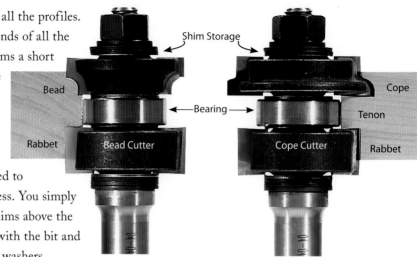

Determine the Length of the Rails and Muntins

Cut every part of the door to exact length in these steps. Use the actual stiles to calculate the precise length of the rails and muntins.

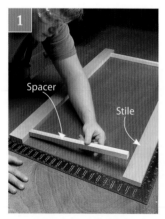

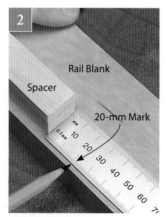

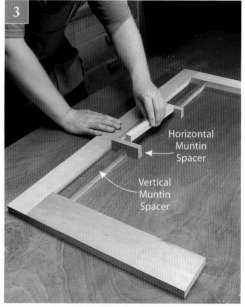

Cut two spacers to spread the stiles to the door's final width. This method prevents you from making a math error with awkward fractions in the next step.

Add the length of two tenons to the spacer and mark this total distance on a rail blank. With the Freud bits, two tenons are equal to 20 mm (about 25/32 in.) Crosscut the rails and horizontal muntin boards to this length.

Use the same process to calculate the vertical muntin boards' length. Position two 3/4-in.-thick blocks to stand in for the 3/4-in.-wide horizontal muntins. Cut two top and bottom spacers the same length. Then cut a middle spacer to fit. Add 20 mm to these spacers to mark and cut the vertical muntin boards.

Cope the Ends

Next, cut tenons on the end grain of every part. Coping the ends before cutting the beads minimizes problems with grain tear-out.

5/8"

Set up the cope cutter. For a 7/8-in.-thick door like this one, raise the bit so the top cutter is 5/8 in. above the table. Position the router table fence so the cutter bearing is perfectly even with the fence or 1/64 in. proud. This assures a full-depth cut, which is necessary for a good fit.

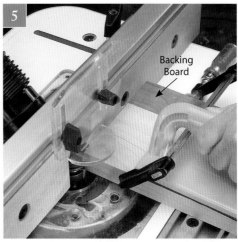

Backing Board

Test cut an extra piece of rail stock. Clamp a backing board to the workpiece to prevent tear-out. Use a push pad to keep the workpiece flat on the table and your fingers out of harm's way.

Shims

Measure the tenon's thickness. It should be 5/16 in. so it fits the mortise made by a 5/16-in. chisel. If the tenon is too thin, add shims above the bearing (see inset). Add the same shims to the bead cutter. When the tenon is correctly sized, cope the ends of all the rails and muntin boards.

Rout the Bead

The bead goes on the long grain of the stiles, rails, and muntins.

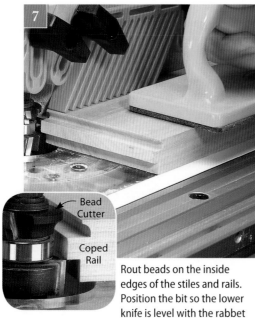

Rout beads on the inside edges of the stiles and rails. Position the bit so the lower knife is level with the rabbet made by the coping cut (see inset). Cut beads on both sides of the muntin boards.

Rip the muntin boards. Use a push block with a stop and hold-down board so you can keep the guard and splitter on your saw. The exact width of this cut—3/4 in.—must be the same as the width of the stand-in muntin blocks you used to calculate the vertical muntin's length in Photo 3.

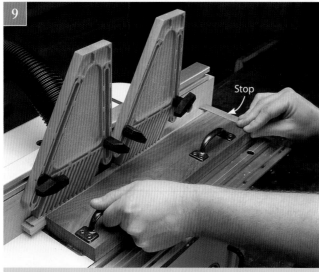

Caution! You must use two featherboards to hold the workpiece square to the table.

Rout the second side of the muntins. Use the same push block as you did on the tablesaw. This time the push block is flipped over and the hold-down removed.

Cut the Mortises

Most routed doors merely have cope and stick joints. Mortise-and-tenon joints strengthen a divided light door to carry the extra weight of the glass.

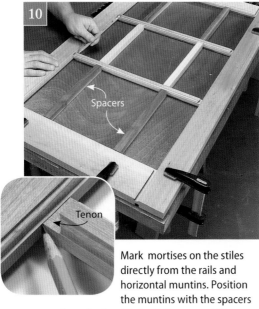

Mark mortises on the stiles directly from the rails and horizontal muntins. Position the muntins with the spacers you made earlier (see Photo 3). Draw pencil lines along both sides of the tenons (see inset). Mark mortises for the vertical muntins in the center of the rails and horizontal muntins.

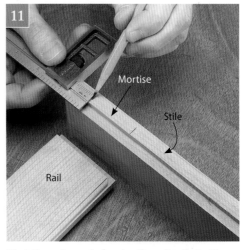

Mark the outer end of each rail mortise that will receive a rail. Typically, this mark is about 3/4 in. from the stile's end.

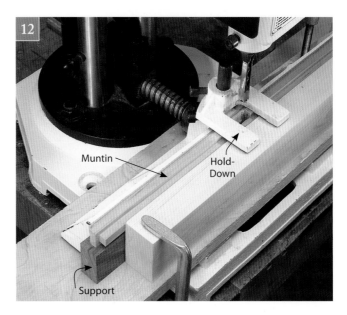

Cut mortises in the muntins halfway through from both sides. Place a support block under the muntin so its top edge is within range of the machine's hold-down. Cut 1/2-in.-deep mortises in the rails and stiles.

Haunch the Rails

Remove the outer part of the rail tenons
to fit the mortises.

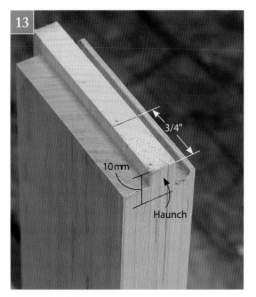

Mark the waste on the tenon's end with
a combination square.

Remove most of the waste with a mortising bit. You
don't have to move the machine's fence. This is the
same setup you used for cutting mortises in the rails
and stiles.

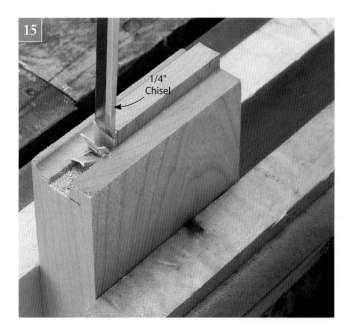

Pare the tenons to width.
Check the fit of all the tenons
in the mortises. File small bevels
on the ends of all the tenons
so they're easier to insert into
the mortises.

Assemble the Door

The entire door must be glued at one time. It's best to work directly on a large, flat assembly table so you can slide each piece home before clamping it.

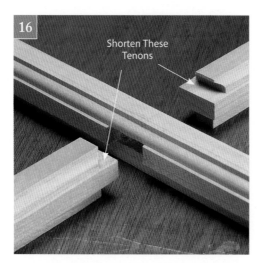

Shorten These Tenons

Cut 1/16 in. off the ends of the vertical muntin tenons. As originally routed, each tenon is slightly over 3/8 in. long. That's too long for the through mortises in the horizontal muntins, which are 3/4 in. wide.

Glue the door. Squeeze-out around the beads can be difficult to clean up, so use a minimum of glue. Sand and finish the door before you install the glass.

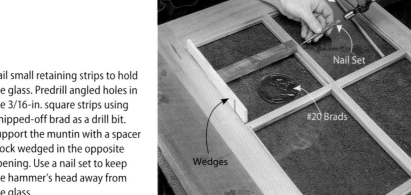

Retaining Strip

Nail Set

#20 Brads

Wedges

Nail small retaining strips to hold the glass. Predrill angled holes in the 3/16-in. square strips using a nipped-off brad as a drill bit. Support the muntin with a spacer block wedged in the opposite opening. Use a nail set to keep the hammer's head away from the glass.

by GEORGE VONDRISKA

Making Cathedral Doors

A COMPLETE RECIPE FOR MAKING BEAUTIFUL CATHEDRAL RAISED-PANEL DOORS

Cathedral raised-panel doors are beautiful, but they can be intimidating to make. After many years of teaching students how to make these doors, I've got a trick or two up my sleeve to simplify the process and remove some of the fear factor. Here's a tried-and-true recipe to help you safely and successfully make beautiful doors.

There are a few specialized tools you must have to make cathedral doors. Start with a suitable router table. It should be equipped with a 2-hp or higher variable-speed router that accepts 1/2-in.-shank router bits. You'll also need a bandsaw or jigsaw for cutting the curves and a set of door-making router bits. The bits and a template set will set you back several hundred dollars, but they are a big part of what makes this technique airtight. The good news is the router bits are not specific to cathedral-top doors; they can be used to make any frame-and-panel door.

You'll need a two-piece matched rail-and-stile set to make the frame. It's easier to get good results with a two-piece set

than with a one-piece reversible bit. With a two-piece set, you feed all the pieces face down. Reversible bits use one arbor with removable cutters. Some parts are machined face up, others face down. This often results in poor alignment between rails and stiles. Plus, it's a hassle to have to change cutters on the arbor. Bits with a 1/2-in. shank will produce less chatter and a smoother cut than those with 1/4-in. shank.

Parts of a Door

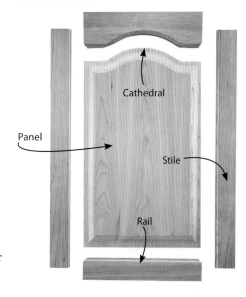

- Cathedral
- Panel
- Stile
- Rail

Recommended Cutters

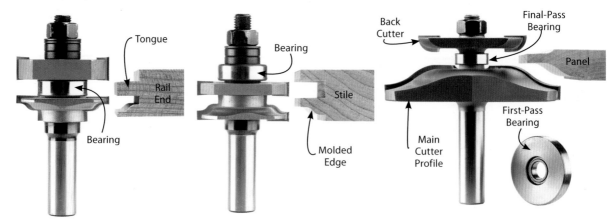

The end-grain cutter is used only on the rail ends and produces the tongue and the mating profile to the molded edge. The depth of cut is controlled by a bearing that rides against the tongue. Mark a number 1 on the end of the shaft with a permanent marker, because it's the first cutter you'll use.

The long-grain cutter is used on the inside edge of all the frame pieces. It makes the groove for both the panel and the tongue on the end of the rails. It also forms the molded edge you see around the inside of the frame. Label this bit with the number 2.

Use a back-cutting panel raiser to make the panel. The main cutter cuts a broad profile in the face of the panel. At the same time, the back cutter sweeps material off the back of the panel to leave a perfectly sized tongue for the groove in the frame. Our favorite bits come with two bearings: The large-diameter bearing is used for the first pass and the small bearing for the final pass.

Make the Frame

First, cut all the frame pieces (see "Sizing a Door," page 86). For a good-looking, stable door, make the frame from straight-grained wood.

Next, on your router table, set up the end-grain cutter for machining the rail ends. Cutting end grain before long grain helps prevent blow-out on the rails. Here's a memory device for you: Machine the Rails before the Stiles, because *R* comes before *S* in the alphabet.

Mark the back of all the frame pieces. They get machined with their good faces down, so you should be looking at the mark on the back for all the cuts.

Note: Run the end-grain and long-grain cutters at full speed on your router.

Recommended Tool: Coping Sled

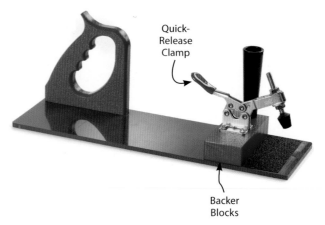

Get a coping sled for making the end-grain cuts on the rails. The sled uses a quick-release clamp to hold the rails with a firm grip. A replaceable backer block keeps the rail square to the fence and backs up the edge of the rail to prevent blow-out.

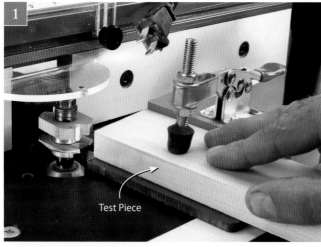

Set the height of the end-grain cutter against a test piece in the coping sled. The cut should leave a shoulder on top of the piece that's twice as thick as the lip on the bottom (see Photo 4). You can tweak the height after a test cut.

Set the fence even with the face of the ball bearing. A straightedge makes quick work of this job.

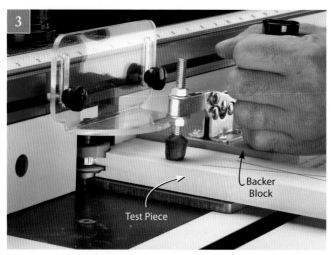

Make a test cut, but don't cut all the way through the test piece. You don't want to cut into the backer block until the bit height is perfect. That way, the block can be used to quickly set the bit height the next time you make doors.

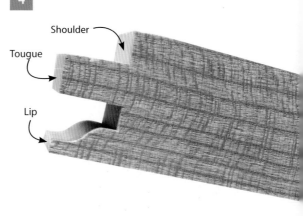

Check the cut. The height of the router bit controls the depth of the shoulder and the thickness of the lip. The tongue size is fixed. The shoulder should be about twice as thick as the lip. In 3/4-in.-thick stock, this works out to a shoulder depth of approximately 3/16 in. Raise or lower the bit as needed and make test cuts until it's right.

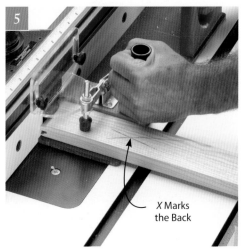

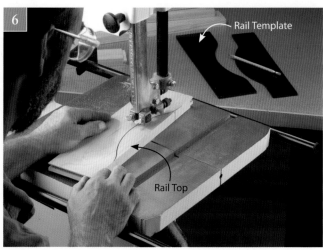

Rout the rail ends. Remember, the back of the board is face up for all cuts. To ensure a uniform cut, keep consistent downward pressure on the sled at all times.

Rough-cut the arch in the top rail. Center the rail template on the top rail with the bottom of the pattern even with the rail's bottom edge. Use a template that is the same length or slightly longer than the rail. Trace the template and use a bandsaw or jigsaw to cut the curve. Stay at least 1/16 in. but no more than 1/8 in. outside the line.

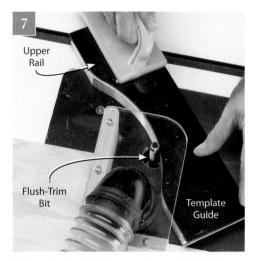

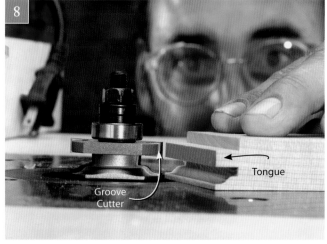

Flush-trim the rail with a template guide and a flush-trim bit. Use double-faced tape to adhere the pattern to the rail. The fence is replaced with a bit cover and starter pin assembly (see Recommended Tool, opposite).

Set the height of the long-grain cutter by aligning the groove cutter with the tongue on the end of a machined rail. The top of the cutter should be even with the top of the tongue.

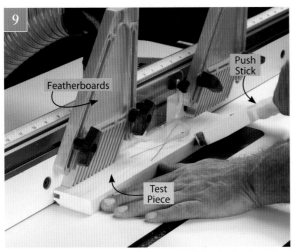

Make a long-grain test cut in a scrap piece. Use featherboards to hold the rail down onto the table and a push stick to drive the piece past the cutter.

Check your work by fitting a rail into the test piece. The faces of both parts should be flush. If they're off by just a little —the thickness of this page, for instance—you're probably OK. A tiny discrepancy like that will easily sand out after assembly. If they're off more than that, raise or lower the bit to correct it. Make test cuts until you've got a good match.

Recommended Tool: Template Set

A cathedral template set is a matched set of rail-and-panel templates. A template can be fastened directly to the material to act as a guide for the flush-trim bit. A set typically covers a range of panel widths, generally from 9-1/2 in. to 22 in. Each pattern has a centering hash mark for locating the pattern on the wood. Sure, with careful layout and bandsaw and drum-sander work, you can make your own patterns, but it's hard to beat the simplicity of commercially made patterns.

Rail Template

Panel Template   Center Mark

Oops!

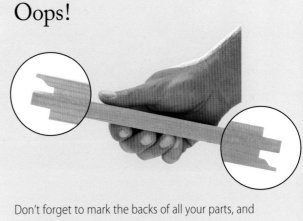

Don't forget to mark the backs of all your parts, and pay attention to the marks. It's very easy to flip a rail and end up with a piece that's no good.

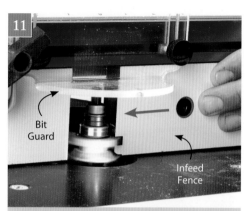

Bit Guard

Infeed Fence

Caution! Make sure your bit guard is in place and the mounting bolts on the fence are just loose enough to let the fence slide easily.

Make a zero-clearance fence by slowly sliding the infeed half of the fence into the spinning bit. This eliminates most of the chipping that can happen on these cuts. You only need the zero-clearance fence on the infeed side.

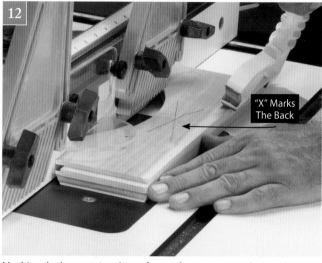

"X" Marks The Back

Machine the long-grain edges of every frame piece, including the straight portions of the arched rail. Make sure the piece is face down. You should be able to see the mark on the back of the piece when you're machining it.

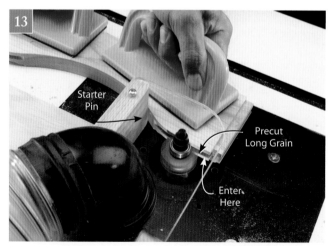

Starter Pin

Precut Long Grain

Enter Here

Begin the arched cut at the precut section of the top rail. First position the rail against the starter pin without contacting the bit. Then pivot the rail into the bit so the bit enters the previous long-grain cut. Caution: Do not allow the bit to contact the end grain, as this typically causes it to grab the rail and ruin the piece.

Bearing

Complete the long-grain cut by pivoting off the starter pin and riding the router-bit bearing through the entire length of the arched rail. Use push blocks to keep consistent downward pressure on the rail throughout the cut.

Make the Panel

Gluing up narrow pieces of wood is the best way to make wide panels. You're more likely to get a panel that won't warp, and it's your chance to exercise some creativity. Look for interesting grain patterns or cool-looking pieces of wood with lots of character.

Large-diameter panel-raising bits must be run slowly, at no more than 12,000 rpm.

Routers with 3-hp motors can easily raise the panel in two passes using the fence to limit the depth of cut. A router whose motor has less than 3 hp may struggle a bit. Use push pads to grip the panel and guide it past the bit.

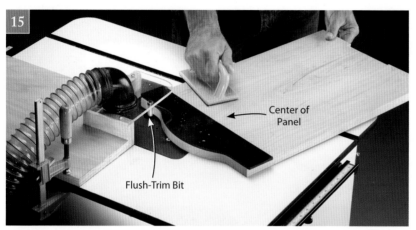

Form the arch on the panel the same way you did the rail, but using the matching panel template. Use a square to make sure the pattern is set square on the panel. Center and trace the pattern, cut outside the line, tape the pattern to the panel and flush-trim the shape.

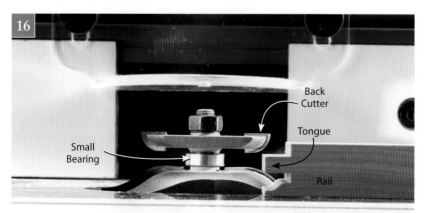

Set the panel-raising bit's height by aligning it with a rail's tongue. "Eyeball" the bit height so the bottom of the back cutter is even with the top of the tongue. Use the bit's small bearing and set the fence 1/4-in. in front of the ball bearing. At this stage, the fence is back in place of the bit cover.

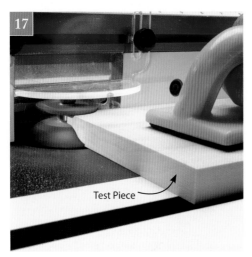

Test Piece

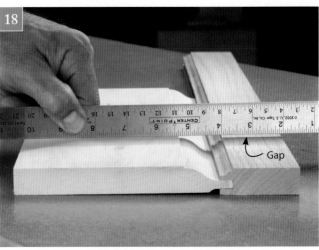

Gap

Make a test cut on the long-grain edge of a piece of scrap. It's easier to cut long grain than end grain, so make your test cuts on a long-grain edge. Make the first pass with the fence about 1/4 in. ahead of the bearing. Set the fence even with the bearing for the second pass.

Check your work by slipping the test piece into the groove and laying a straightedge across the face. The panel and the frame face should be flush. In this case, the gap means the bit is set too high. Adjust and test the bit height until it's right. When the correct bit height is established, replace the small bearing with the large one.

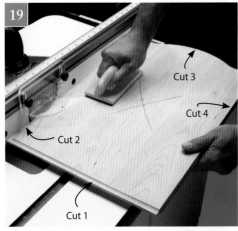

Cut 3

Cut 4

Cut 2

Cut 1

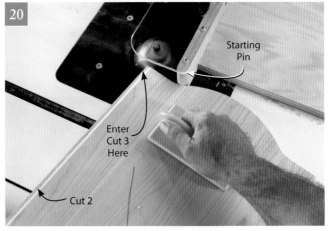

Starting Pin

Enter Cut 3 Here

Cut 2

Make the first pass on the panel with the face of the fence set even with the large bearing. The first cut is made on the panel's bottom edge. Rotate the panel counterclockwise and make the second cut on the long-grain edge. Keep the panel moving in one continuous motion to prevent burning. Cuts 3 and 4 will require different setups.

Set up to cut the panel arch (Cut 3) by removing the fence and clamping the bit cover and starting pin in place. Turn on the router and position the arch against the starting pin without contacting the bit. Rip the panel to width, but don't cut it to length until after you've flush-trimmed the arch on top, just in case you have a problem with the flush-trimming step. Mark the back of the panel to remind you to keep it face down on the router table.

Start the cut by easing the panel into the bit so the bit enters at the previously cut corner. At this point, the arch is in contact with both the starting pin and the bearing on the router bit.

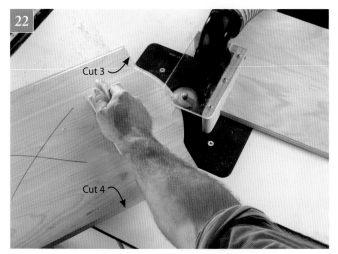

Rout the arch by pivoting off the starting pin so the panel is only contacting the router-bit bearing. Finish the arch, reposition the fence so it's even with the bearing and make Cut 4 on the remaining long-grain edge. Replace the large bearing with the small one and repeat the process (Photos 19 through 22) for the final pass.

Tips

- If you're making a door with rails and stiles less than 2 in. wide, it's easier and safer to work with pieces wide enough to make two back-to-back pieces. After all the machining is done, rip the stock down the middle to create a pair of stiles or rails.

- Practice making a door with an easy-to-machine material, such as poplar or pine. Keep a successfully made door, dry-assembled only, so you can use the parts for future setups.

- Make extra pieces, just in case. Rails are especially easy to goof up. You'll appreciate having a spare ready to go if you need it.

- Use straight-grained material for the frame and more open-grained pieces for the panel.

- Prefinish the panel before you assemble the door.

Recommended Gear: Bit Cover

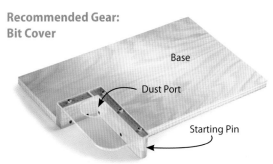

A shop-made bit cover with a starter pin is essential, because the arched shapes can't be cut with a fence. The starter pin acts as a fulcrum for easing the arched rail and panel into the router bit. The cover protects your hands and provides dust collection. The large plywood base allows you to clamp the cover to your router table.

Assemble the Door

Sand all the pieces before putting the door together. Be careful when sanding the long-grain profile on the stiles. If you sand too much, the stiles won't mate with the rails the way they should.

Prefinish the panel to guarantee the entire panel is coated with finish. That way you won't have unfinished edges peeking out of the frame when the panel shrinks in winter. Prefinishing also prevents glue squeeze-out from gluing the panel to the frame, which would prevent the panel from floating in the frame. A glued-in, solid-wood panel is bound to crack as it tries to expand and contract with seasonal changes.

Have everything you need ready before applying the first drop of glue. Glue dries fast, and you don't want the glue to start setting up while you're running around the shop looking for a clamp.

Speaking of clamps, use good ones. Sure, you can make almost any clamp work, but parallel jaw clamps are the best by far. They stay dead flat, even under clamp pressure. If you only spring for one pair—and glue a kitchen full of doors one door at a time—you won't regret it.

Glue in sequence from 1 to 5. Start with a stile and the top rail. Add the panel, then the bottom rail, and capture it all with the last stile. Keep the edge of the rail dead even with the end of the stile.

When you apply glue to the rail ends, make sure the entire profile is covered except for the areas just above and below the groove. This helps prevent getting glue on the panel.

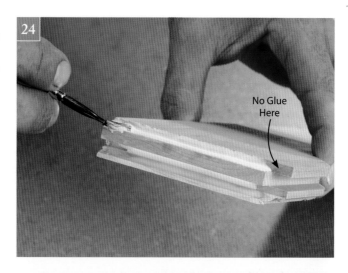

No Glue Here

Clamp the door gently. It doesn't take much pressure to pull the rails and stiles together. Excessive clamping can bow the door. Measure the diagonals to make sure the door is square. If it's not, loosen the clamps and rack them in the same direction as the longer of the two diagonals. Tighten the clamps, and recheck the diagonal.

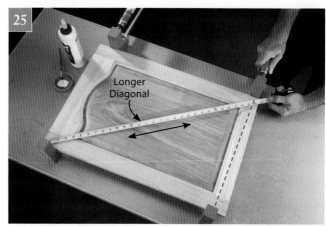

Longer Diagonal

Tip

Anti-Rattle Snakes

Solid-wood panels expand and contract seasonally. When they're at their smallest, they can rattle within the frame. You can take the rattle out with these silicone strips. Make them by squeezing 1/8-in.-dia. beads of silicone caulk onto a piece of wax paper. After the caulk dries, peel off the strips and cut them into 1-in. lengths. Set these into the grooves before you assemble the door. They'll provide a cushion that allows the panel to expand but not rattle.

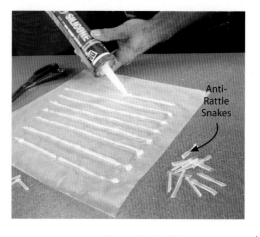

Anti-Rattle Snakes

Sizing a Door

Before you can calculate the lengths of the rails and stiles, you have to know how the door will fit over or into the cabinet opening. If the door will lay over the opening, it's called an overlay door. You must know the amount of overlay to make your rail and stile calculations. The size of the overlay —how much bigger the door is than the opening—can be affected by the hardware you use. So, get the hardware before you build your door.

If the door will be set inside the opening, it's called an inset door. To calculate your stile and rail size on an inset door, you need to know the gap size between the door and the cabinet (usually about 1/32 in.). Many cabinetmakers cut the parts to fit the opening exactly and then trim the assembled door to create the gap.

Figure A: Sizing Stiles and Rails

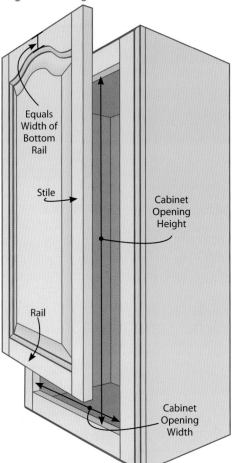

Equals Width of Bottom Rail

Stile

Rail

Cabinet Opening Height

Cabinet Opening Width

Calculate the stile length by measuring the height of the opening and either adding the overlay amount or subtracting the inset gap's width.

Calculate the rail length by first measuring the width of the opening. Add the overlay or subtract the inset gap amount; this gives you the door's overall width. Now, subtract the width of the two stiles and then add the length of the two tongues on the ends of the rail (Fig. B).

Determine the width of the arched rail. First, measure the depth of the arch in the rail using the appropriate template guide. Make the top rail wide enough so that after the arch is cut out, the thinnest part of the rail top equals the width of the bottom rail.

Determine the panel size by dry-assembling the frame and measuring from groove bottom to groove bottom. Make the panel 1/8-in. smaller in both length and width to allow for expansion. On many cutters, the shoulder on the frame's face is aligned with the bottom of the groove (Fig. C). This allows you to simply measure from shoulder to shoulder on the dry-fit frame.

Figure B: Rail End

Figure C: Stile Cross Section

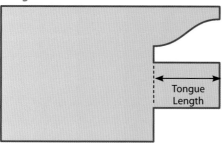

Shoulder

Tongue Length

Groove Bottom

Measure the tongue length on the rails. You need this number to calculate the rail length. When you figure out the dimension for your router bits (it can vary from manufacturer to manufacturer), keep it—you'll use it for every set of doors you make with that cutter.

To determine the panel size, you first need to know the distances from groove bottom to groove bottom in the assembled frame. Most cutters align the shoulder on the frame's face with the groove bottom. This allows you to take the necessary measurements right on top of the assembled frame (see Fig. A photo).

Figure D: Bit Cover and Starting Pin

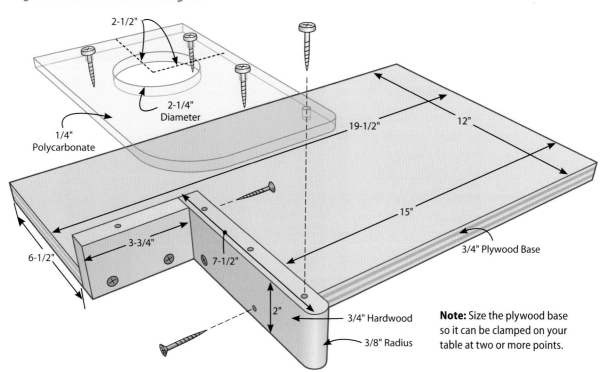

2-1/2"

2-1/4" Diameter

1/4" Polycarbonate

19-1/2"

12"

15"

3-3/4"

6-1/2"

7-1/2"

2"

3/4" Plywood Base

3/4" Hardwood

3/8" Radius

Note: Size the plywood base so it can be clamped on your table at two or more points.

by BRAD HOLDEN

Making Curved Doors

KERFKORE FLEXIBLE PANELS HANDLE CURVES WITH EASE

Curved doors and panels add elegance to any project, especially kitchen cabinets. Making these complicated parts requires careful planning and building. The task can be made much easier by using a flexible panel product called Kerfkore (see photo, right). It follows the same principle that cabinetmakers use when they saw multiple kerfs on the back of a piece of plywood to make it flexible. A disadvantage to this saw-kerfing method is the risk of the face veneer cracking or kinking at the kerfs, spoiling the curve's smooth surface. Kerfcore's advantage is that that the kerfing is done for you. Its flexible paper backing provides a smooth surface to attach your veneer.

There are several important tricks and techniques to working with Kerfkore but it's a surprisingly easy material to work with. I'll walk you through the main steps of making a curved door with Kerfkore from layout to final trimming. Information on using Kerfkore in other applications can be found at the Web site www.kerfkore.com.

Doors made with Kerfkore have a smooth, even curve.

PHOTO COURTESY OF ROBB YOUNG'S FINE WOODWORKING HONOLULU, HAWAII, WWW.ROBBYOUNGSFINEWOODWORKING.COM

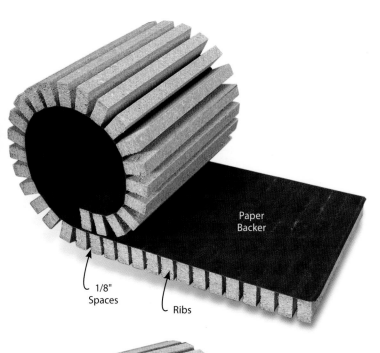

Paper Backer

1/8" Spaces

Ribs

Kerfkore flexes easily in both directions.

What is Kerfkore?

Kerfkore is a very flexible panel made of 3/8-in.-wide ribs spaced 1/8 in. apart on a paper backer sheet. The spaces between the ribs allows the board to flex. The flexible backer sheet provides a smooth surface for veneering. The ribs in different Kerfkore products are made of particleboard, lauan plywood, poplar plywood, MDF, fire-rated treated particleboard, or lightweight styrene foam. These different cores have different weights, strengths, and screw-holding characteristics. The particleboard core works well for general-purpose doors, such as those for kitchen cabinets.

Kerfkore with paper backer on both sides is also available. This makes the material more rigid and somewhat easier to handle and enables you to create a curve that turns into a straight run. To make the two-sided variety bend, you cut the backer on one side with a utility knife where you need the bend to occur.

Kerfkore comes in 4-ft. by 8-ft. sheets in 1/4-in., 3/8-in., 1/2-in., 5/8-in., and 3/4-in. thicknesses.

1

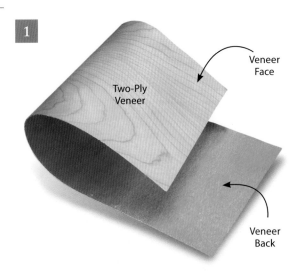

Two-Ply
Veneer

Veneer
Face

Veneer
Back

Pick Your Veneer

Your three main veneer choices are two-ply wood veneer (shown here), phenolic-backed (plastic-laminate) wood veneer, or vertical-grade plastic laminate. The two-ply veneer is the most flexible of the three and is easily cut with a utility knife or scissors. The phenolic-backed veneer and plastic laminate must be sawn or scored and snapped. The cut edge of the two-ply veneer leaves a dark line that may show on your finished door, depending on the wood species and the finish you apply. The phenolic-backed veneer and plastic laminate both leave a black edge line.

2

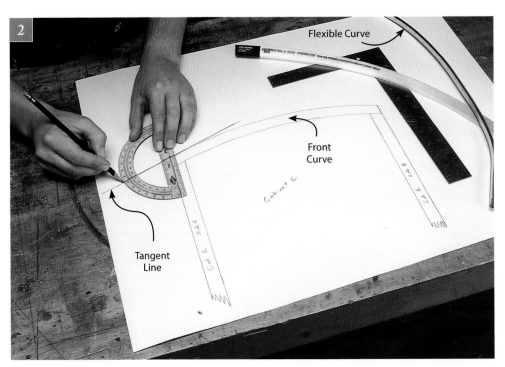

Flexible Curve

Front
Curve

Tangent
Line

Make a Full-Size Drawing

Use a top-view drawing to determine the size of the Kerfkore panel and the angles at the edges. The width of the Kerfkore should be the outer circumference of the curve minus 1-1/2 in. to 2 in. for the solid-wood edges. The measurement is easy to take using a flexible curve.

Calculate the angles of the edges by drawing a line tangent to the front curve at the corner of the door and then measure the angle with a protractor.

Apply the Front Veneer First

Use contact cement and work flat when applying the first sheet of veneer. Working flat may seem odd, but when you do so, the contact cement remains flexible and a good bond is ensured. The panel will gain a bit of stiffness but will remain flexible enough to form to its final shape later on.

Front Side of Door

Contact Cement

Add Solid-Wood Edges for Strength, Appearance

Solid-wood strips provide durable finished edges when the door is done. Each strip can be up to 1 in. wide. Leave a 1/8-in. gap between the solid-wood strip and the adjacent rib to maintain maximum flexibility. Attach the strip with contact cement. After the edge strips are attached, use a small router and a shop-made edge guide (Photo 8) to trim the veneer flush around the entire panel.

Solid-Wood Edge

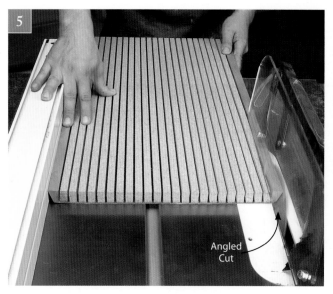

Cut the Edges to the Required Angle

It's easier and safer to cut the angles on the panel while it's flat, rather than after it has been curved. Cut at the angles you measured on the full-size drawing (Photo 2). The panel is sufficiently stiff at this stage that it saws much like a normal piece of plywood.

Attach the Back Veneer with Yellow Wood Glue

Yellow glue dries stiff and helps the curved door hold its shape. The folks at Kerfkore recommend yellow glue for both two-ply and phenolic-backed veneer. The grain on the back of two-ply veneer runs 90 degrees to its face side and adds stiffness to the door when the glue dries.

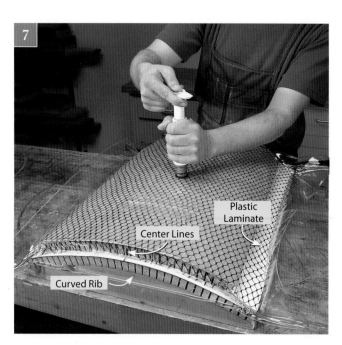

Attach the Back Veneer with a Vacuum Press

A curved form—made from two curved ribs and a spare piece of Kerfkore covered with plastic laminate—provide the shape. A vacuum bag provides clamping pressure.

Mark centerlines on the form and on the ends of the door. Line up the marks prior to clamping to ensure the curved door ends up straight after the glue dries. With the whole assembly in a vacuum bag, pump the air out. Netting in the bag prevents air pockets from forming. Let the glue dry completely before you remove the door.

Trim the Curved Edges

This shop-made edge guide (see photos, below) simplifies routing the veneer on the curved edges. The guide fence has an angled opening and clearance slot that allow it to trim around the curved overhanging veneer. It works equally well on the convex and the concave sides of the door. You can use either a ball-bearing-guided straight bit or a standard straight bit with this guide. The edge guide is slotted so its fence can be adjusted flush with the edge of the router bit.

Veneer the Ends and Trim Flush

Apply veneer to the end with contact cement or yellow glue and trim flush. When all edges and veneers are trimmed, the doors can be installed. Hanging a curved door is not difficult. Butt hinges go on the same way as they do with a flat door. For European-style hinges, support the door on the drill-press table so the hinge-hole drill bit drills square to the surface of the door. If the hinge-cup screws land in a gap between the wood ribs, squeeze in some epoxy glue as a filler and anchor.

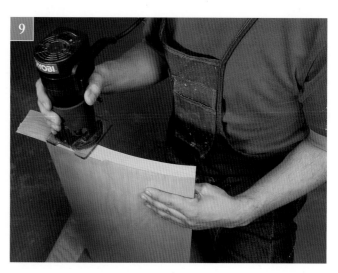

by ANDY RAE

Flush-Fit Cabinet Doors

A SIMPLE JIG FOR A PERFECT FIT

Flush-fit or inset doors are found in a wide variety of furniture styles from Philadelphia highboys, to Shaker cupboards, to sleek contemporary pieces. The greatest challenge in hanging a flush-fit door is achieving an even gap between the doors and the cabinet while accurately locating the mortises for the hinges. After all, there are no adjustment screws on butt hinges and there's no door lip to cover the cabinet opening.

The good news is that a few savvy techniques and a nifty jig (Photo 1) will have you hanging these doors like a pro. I'll show you how to achieve the perfect fit every time. We'll even cover fixing goof-ups.

Fit the Cabinet Hinges First

First things first. Whether you're making a cabinet with a face frame or one without, cut the mortises for the hinge leaves in the frame or case sides before assembly. This saves hassles later when rails or cabinet tops can get in the way. I use the same technique for mortising the case as I do for the doors.

Make the Doors

I always dimension my doors so they are the exact size of my case opening. This approach lets me fine-tune the fit of the doors to the cabinet once it's built.

Flat and square doors prevent untold headaches later. Be sure to work on a flat surface when you glue up your doors, and center the clamping pressure over the joints. Before the glue sets, check each door for square by measuring its diagonals.

Trim the Door to Fit the Case

At first the doors won't fit into the case opening because there's no gap. That's OK. This two-step trimming procedure allows you to get the perfect fit:

The first step is to joint all four edges of each door (Photo 2). Periodically check the fit, and joint until you have

a gap of roughly 1/16 in. all around between the door and the case.

The second step is to fine-tune the fit of the doors to the case. Position each door into the case on a pair of shop-made hangers (Photo 1 and Fig. A).

Figure A: Door Hanger Jig

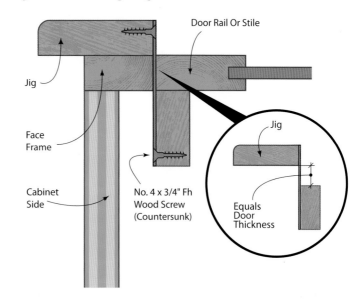

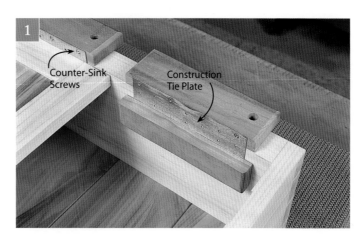

Shop-made door hangers hold the doors in place so you can scribe for a perfect fit. They're constructed from two blocks of hardwood and a metal tie plate. Tie plates are used to join house framing and are available from home centers.

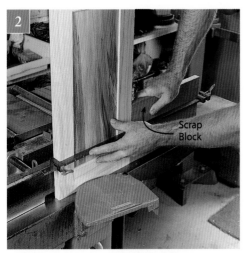

First, trim the edges on the jointer. Set the infeed table for a light cut (1/32 in. or less), and joint all four edges. A scrap block steadies the door and prevents end-grain tearout.

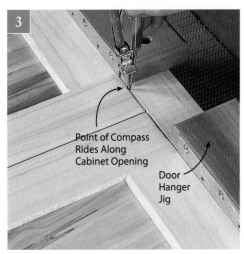

Position the doors on hangers and check the fit of the doors to the case. The hangers hold the doors flush with the cabinet face and establish a 1/6-in. gap. Set the compass to the largest gap, then mark around the doors with the compass.

Chances are, your doors won't fit the opening with precise, even gaps all around. To make the gaps perfect, use a compass to mark the doors (Photo 3). The hangers prevent the compass from scribing across the entire width of the door, so use a straightedge to finish.

Next, clamp the door in a bench vise and trim to your marks with a hand plane (Photo 4). For paired doors, plane a slight back bevel on the stiles where they meet.

Installing the Hinges

Position the doors back into the case and mark the locations of each hinge mortise with a sharp knife (Photo 5.)

Back at the bench, square your knife marks across the edge of the stile with a square and a sharp pencil. Set a marking gauge to the desired width of the hinge (Photo 6). Then mark the long-grain shoulder of the mortise (Photo 7).

A router makes for fast, accurate work when cutting mortises. I use a 1/4-in. straight bit to cut all my hinge mortises because the smaller diameter lets me get very close to the inside corners of the mortise. Set the height of the bit to the thickness of a hinge leaf (Photo 8).

Clamp the door firmly in a bench vise and secure a scrap board to the benchtop. The scrap board's surface must be flush with the edge of the door to support the router base. Now rout the mortise freehand (Photo 9).

Plane the edges to your compass marks to true the doors. Use a sharp bench plane set for a light cut. Maintain a square edge by checking your cuts with a square.

Mark for hinges by positioning the door into the opening with the door hangers. With the hinge stile tight against the case, transfer the shoulder locations of each hinge mortise with a sharp marking knife.

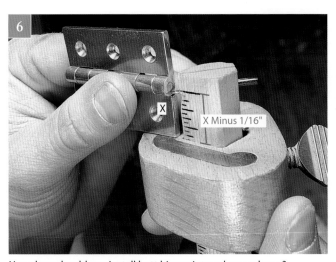

How deep should you install butt hinges into a door and case? The rule of thumb is to measure from the center point of the hinge barrel to the outside edge of one leaf, then subtract about 1/16 in. This layout ensures that the door won't bind on the face of the cabinet when opened.

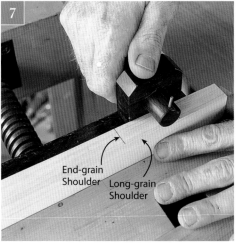

Scribe the long-grain shoulder with the marking gauge to finish the hinge mortise layout.

Set the bit depth by laying a hinge leaf on the router's baseplate. Route a test mortise on a piece of scrap and check for fit. The hinge leaf should be flush with the top of the mortise. A 1/4-in. straight-tip bit is a good choice for routing the mortise.

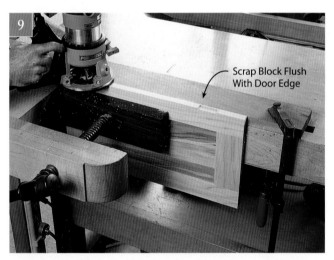

Rout the hinge mortise freehand, staying about 1/16 in. inside your layout lines. For a really clean cut, move the router in the opposite direction that you would normally rout: a technique called climb cutting. Routing in this manner prevents tearout, and it's easy to control the router because the cut isn't very deep and the bit diameter is relatively small. A scrap block clamped to the bench steadies the router's baseplate.

Square the mortise with a razor-sharp chisel (Photo 10).

You'll need to drill pilot holes for the hinge screws before securing the new hinges to the door and the case. To make the drilling job foolproof, use a self-centering bit (Photo 11).

Hanging the Doors

With the hinges attached to each door, press the loose leaves into their respective mortises in the case and install the screws. Now open and close the doors and inspect the fit. Your doors should swing as smooth as silk, with the doors flush to the face of the cabinet, and even gaps all around. If you notice some unevenness, a little judicious sanding with some 180-grit sandpaper wrapped around a block can usually fix the problem. Once you're satisfied with the fit, mark the doors for knobs or pulls and install these along with your favorite catch hardware. Case closed.

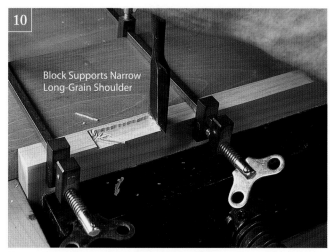

Block Supports Narrow Long-Grain Shoulder

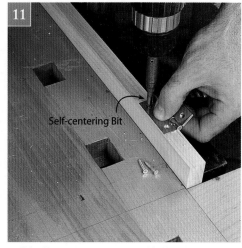

Self-centering Bit

Shave the shoulders by chopping lightly with a sharp chisel. It's best to sneak up on your layout line, making several thin cuts until you reach the end-grain shoulder line. Clamp a block behind the long-grain shoulder to support this delicate area and take multiple cuts until you reach the shoulder line. Finish up by paring into the corners to clean up any left-over slivers of wood.

Drill for hinge screws using a self-centering drill bit. Lay each hinge in its mortise and drill through the hinge and into the door. Rub a little wax onto the screw threads to lubricate them before driving the screws home.

Tip Brass screws break easily! Use the same size steel screws first and install the brass screws after fitting and finishing are complete.

Oops!

Uh-oh! We accidentally trimmed too much off one edge of a door. Luckily, it was a long-grain edge and there's a simple fix. Re-joint the edge, then glue on a thin strip to increase the door's width. The strip should match the stile in grain and color and be slightly oversize in width and length. Trim it to fit after the glue dries. You'll never see the fix!

Repair Strip

by TOM CASPAR

Making Lipped Drawers with a Dovetail Jig

THESE STYLISH DRAWERS ARE EASIER THAN YOU THINK

You can do more with your half-blind dovetail jig than meets the eye. You've probably used it to make drawers with plain, inset fronts, but it's really quite simple to make lipped drawer fronts, too. Even though most dovetail jigs are basically the same, some of their manuals don't go into much detail about how to make this variation of the basic drawer (they often call it a rabbeted drawer, which is confusing). Whatever kind of jig you have, here's a foolproof process for making lipped drawers from beginning to end.

If this is your first time out with a dovetail jig, try making some standard half-blind joints to familiarize yourself with the process and to fine-tune the settings of your jig. Make a sample

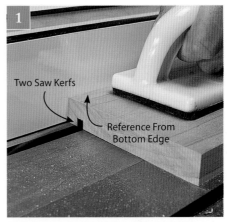

Cut rabbets to form lips on the top and ends of the drawer front (usually there's no lip on the bottom). The precise width of the rabbets affects the fit of the drawer front in its opening. Fine-tune the fence setting so there is 1/16 in. or less total side play between the inside of the drawer front and the sides of the case.

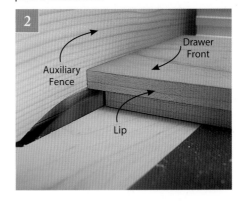

Cut a groove for the drawer bottom in all the drawer parts. If you're using plywood or hardboard for drawer bottoms, the groove must be slightly less than 1/4-in. wide for a good fit. Fine-tune the width of the groove by making two cuts with a standard saw blade. Cut a single saw-kerf groove in all the drawer parts first, then move the saw fence over a bit and groove all the parts a second time.

corner and use it to work out these two important design details:

Ideal drawer widths. Design the case around the drawers. Figure out the width of the drawer sides first, then size the openings of your case on paper. Why? I think drawer sides look best when there's a half-pin at the bottom and the top (Fig. B, page 105). Their ideal widths are multiples of one number: the distance between pin centers. That's typically 7/8 in., but some jigs are slightly different.

Location of drawer-bottom groove. No matter how many different drawer sizes you're making, for workshop efficiency it's best to have this groove in the same location

for every drawer. Center the groove on the lowest socket of the drawer front. On your sample corner, mark the edges that you placed against the jig's stops. Measure the distance from that edge to the center of the first socket.

Once you've worked out the details, build the case. Then cut all your drawer parts to fit the actual box. Make the sides and back the same width. The drawer fronts are wider than the sides by the height of the lip, generally about 1/4 in. The fronts are longer than the backs by the width of two lips. Finally, set up your tablesaw to cut a 1/4-in.-deep drawer-bottom groove and follow Photos 1 through 10.

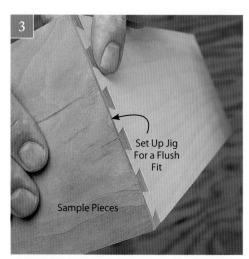

3

Set Up Jig For a Flush Fit

Sample Pieces

Check the fit of sample dovetails made with your jig. Use the same species of wood as your drawer parts for test pieces. Wood that's too soft gives a false reading.

Adjust the router bit up or down until you make two parts that fit together with hand pressure alone.

Adjust the jig's template in and out until you make two parts that fit flush. The position of the template affects the depth of the sockets.

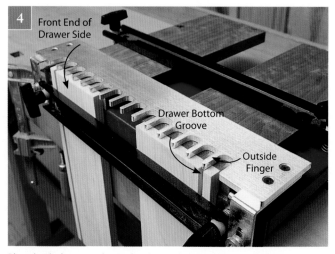

4 Front End of Drawer Side

Drawer Bottom Groove

Outside Finger

Place both drawer sides in the dovetail jig, inside out and front side up. Use the groove in the drawer bottom as a reference guide. It faces toward you and lines up with an outside finger of the dovetail template.

The bottom edge of every drawer part butts up against the stops on the jig.

Rout dovetails in the drawer sides. Move the router from left to right for best results.

Use backer boards behind the drawer sides to prevent the backs of the tails from chipping out.

Place the drawer front in the jig. One end of the board is cut on the right side of the jig. The other end is cut on the left side. Again, use the groove as a reference guide. This time it lines up with the outside slot of the template.

Figure A: Rabbeted Spacer Board

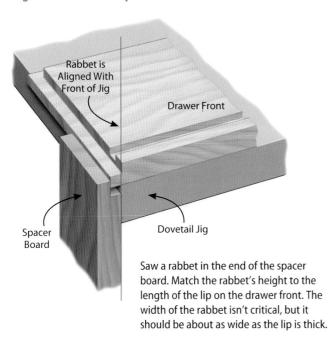

Saw a rabbet in the end of the spacer board. Match the rabbet's height to the length of the lip on the drawer front. The width of the rabbet isn't critical, but it should be about as wide as the lip is thick.

A rabbeted spacer board makes setup a breeze.

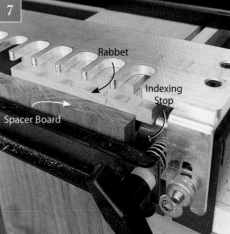

Align the drawer front using a shop-made spacer board (Fig. A, at left). The end grain of the rabbet must be exactly in line with the front edge of the jig so the dovetail is cut to the correct depth.

Cut dovetails in both ends of the drawer front.

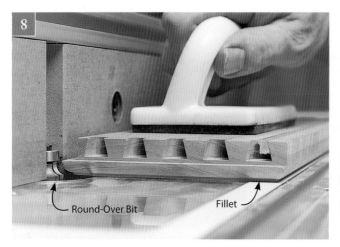

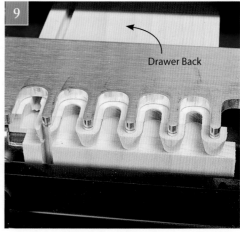

Rout a profile on all four sides of the drawer front. A 1/4-in. round-over is typical. Raising the bit up a little to create a fillet adds an attractive shadow line.

You really can't rout this profile before cutting the dovetails because you need square edges (not round ones!) on the sides of the drawer front. These sides bump up against thin indexing stops on most dovetail jigs (see Photo 7).

Dovetail one drawer side and back as a pair, making a standard half-blind joint. As in Photo 4, one pair is placed in the left-hand side of the jig and the other pair in the right-hand side. You won't get parts mixed up if you remember that the grooves always go nearest the stops of the jig.

Sand all the inside faces of the drawer before gluing.

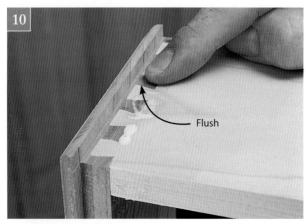

Glue up the drawer with care. The drawer side and rabbet should end up flush.

The lip of the drawer prevents you from easily evening up the joint with a plane or belt sander, so the time it took to set up a perfect joint in the beginning pays off now!

Figure B: Sizing Drawer Sides

A half-tail at the top of a drawer looks awkward and unbalanced. To avoid an unbalanced look, check out the dovetail spacing of your jig first, then design your case. However, both joints will be plenty strong.

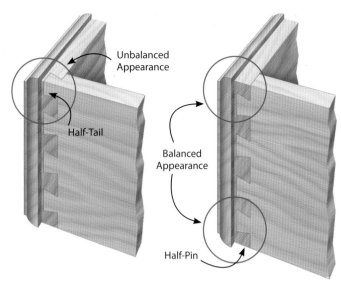

Unbalanced Appearance

Half-Tail

Balanced Appearance

Half-Pin

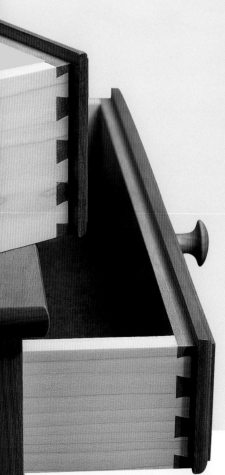

Lipped vs. Standard Drawers

The idea of putting a lip around a drawer probably dates from the early 1800s. While there's no record of why cabinetmakers went to the considerable trouble of adding lips to drawers, here are our guesses. All of these reasons are as valid now as they were 200 years ago.

Lips make fitting easier. Standard drawers require careful measurement and individual fitting to minimize the clearance gaps around their sides and tops. Lipped drawers always appear to fit well, no matter how large the clearance gaps.

Lips are drawer stoppers. They prevent the drawer from going too far back into the case. Stoppers for standard drawers can be awkward to make and install. Not so for lipped drawers. Thin, fragile lips, however, may break off if a heavy drawer is slammed too hard.

Lips seal out smoke, dust and vermin. Homemakers of 200 years ago must have appreciated a new design feature that would help keep clothes cleaner.

Hinges and Hardware

The many available options, including hinges, drawer slides, pulls, shelf supports, and tightening, make hardware selection a mind-spinning experience. The selection and installation information covered in this chapter will enable you to make an informed decision. Once you understand the differences in hardware, you'll be able to choose from the exciting varieties to find something perfect for your application. However (and this is a very big however) it's important to purchase your hardware before you build your project. Relying on the specifications from a catalog is no replacement for physically testing hardware prior to finalizing the design and construction of your cabinet. You might be able to get away with using some types of standardized hardware, but you're inviting trouble if you haven't actually used the hardware before. So buy and test first so you avoid joining countless numbers of woodworkers who have had to painfully modify or rebuild their cabinets in order to make the hardware work.

by TIM JOHNSON

How to Hang Inset Doors

INSTALL BUTT HINGES PERFECTLY AND ESTABLISH CONSISTENT, SLENDER MARGINS

Nothing shows skillful craftsmanship like an inset door with elegant hinges and eye-pleasing margins. This challenging job leaves no room for error: Uneven surfaces and unsightly gaps will tell the tale if the hinges, door, and frame don't fit precisely. Like mastering hand-cut dovetails, successfully hanging inset doors on mortised butt hinges is a woodworking milestone.

I'll show you a three-step method for installing inset doors that produces great results every time. First, you match the door to the opening. Then you rout mortises for the hinges. And finally, you create uniform, attractive margins between the door and frame. Of course, you can skip the mortising step altogether by choosing different hinges.

To complete the job, you'll need a couple simple jigs, a mortising bit, and a laminate trimmer. A laminate trimmer is a compact router that's a really handy addition to any woodworking shop. (If you don't own a laminate trimmer, this is a great excuse to buy one.)

Round out your door-installing arsenal with a pair of secret weapons—a plastic laminate sample swiped from the home center and a double-bearing flush-trim router bit. This great new bit should be a fixture in every woodworking shop.

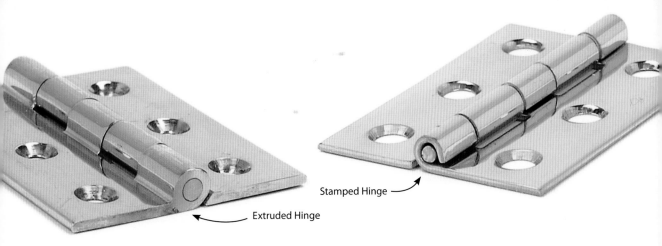

Stamped Hinge

Extruded Hinge

Choose Hinges

Your first task is to choose between extruded (also referred to as drawn or cast) or stamped hinges (see photos, above). Extruded hinges are machined and drilled, so there's virtually no play between the knuckles or around the hinge pin. Stamped hinges are made from thinner stock. Their leaves are bent to form the knuckles that surround the pin. Extruded hinges will last longer, because their knuckles have more bearing surface.

I often use stamped hinges because they cost about one-third as much as extruded hinges and they're available at most hardware stores. They work fine in most situations. Examine stamped hinges carefully before buying. If you notice large gaps between the knuckles and vertical play between the two hinge leaves, keep looking. Be aware that some stamped hinges are brass plated rather than solid brass. Hinges with loose pins make it easy to remove and reinstall the door, but they aren't widely available.

Friction-Fit the Door

I make each door about 1/32 in. larger than its opening. Then I trim it to fit squarely and snugly. First I joint the latch stile until the door slips between the face frame's stiles without binding. Then I check the door's fit: While holding the hinge stile flush against the face frame, I butt the door's top edge against the frame's upper rail. If no gap appears, the door and opening are square. Then I joint the door's top and bottom until the door wedges into the opening—I want a friction fit, so the door stays put.

If the door or the face frame are out of square, I true them by tapering the door's hinge stile. I mark the end that needs to be tapered while I hold the door in position (Photo 1). If the gap along the top appears above the hinge stile, as in the photo, the side's taper increases from top to bottom. If the top's gap appears above the latch stile, the side's taper runs in the opposite direction. The taper increases from zero at one end to the width of the top's gap at the other

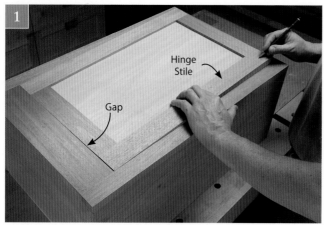

True an out-of-square door by tapering the side, rather than the end. The side is longer, so the taper will be more gradual and less noticeable. In this case, making the hinge stile narrower at the marked end will eliminate the gap at the top.

Taper the side with a straight board and a flush-trim bit. Position the board so it's offset by the width of the gap at the marked end and flush at the other end. Routing this taper eliminates the guesswork associated with creating tapers with a jointer.

Figure A: Hinge-Mortising Jig

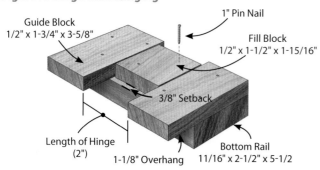

This jig requires a mortising bit with a top-mounted bearing (Photo 6). Both guide blocks are perpendicular to the bottom rail. The distance between the guide blocks is the length of the hinge. The fill block sets the mortises' width; its setback ensures through mortises.

Figure B: Hinge Projection Guide

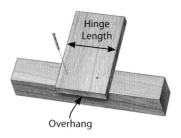

This guide positions the hinge so the center of the barrel projects 1/32 in. beyond the frame and door. Determine the exact overhang by trial and error. It depends on the thickness of your stock and the width of the hinge leaf (Photo 4).

Figure C: Mortise Depth

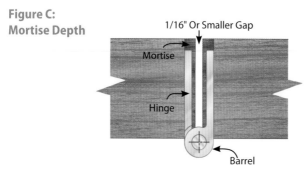

Your mortises should create a gap of 1/16 in. or slightly less between the door and the frame. Usually, this means the hinge leaves must be recessed slightly below the surface. If they're flush, the gap will be too wide. If they're too deep, the gap will disappear and the door will bind.

Calculate the hinge mortise depth by subtracting 1/16 in. from the hinge barrel diameter and dividing the remainder in half.

end. If the top's gap is wider than 1/16 in., I taper both the side and the end, removing one half of the gap from each edge.

Routing is one way to taper the stile (Photo 2). You could also use a hand plane or your jointer. Just make sure the taper runs the full length and the tapered edge is perpendicular to the door's face. When both the hinge stile and top edge fit properly without any gaps, trim the bottom edge so the door fits snugly in the opening.

Before you install the hinges, make sure the screws' heads recess fully in the chamfered holes in the hinge leaves. Amazingly, the brass screws supplied with brass hinges often don't fit. If that's the case, you'll have to deepen the screw-hole chamfers or use smaller screws.

Brass screws are delicate. The heads strip easily or break off, leaving the shaft buried in the wood. Avoid trouble with broken brass screws by threading the pilot holes with steel screws, which are much more durable. Install the brass screws only once, after the piece is completely finished. Or forget brass screws altogether and leave the steel screws in.

Rout the Mortises

Make two jigs, one for routing the hinge mortises (Fig. A, left; Photo 3) and the other to position the hinge in the mortise (Fig. B, left; Photo 4). Then rout test mortises to dial in the depth of cut (Fig. C, left; Photo 5). Laminate samples make perfect gap testers for frame-and-panel doors with stiles and rails up to 2 in. wide; these samples are usually slightly less than 1/16 in. thick. Doors with wider frame

Use the hinges to make your mortising jig. This guarantees that the hinges will perfectly fit the mortises. After installing the guide blocks, add the fill block to provide continuous support for the router.

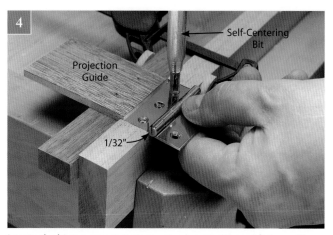

Locate the hinges on a test piece, using a projection guide to position the center of the barrel 1/32 in. out from the board's face. Drill pilot holes using a self-centering bit.

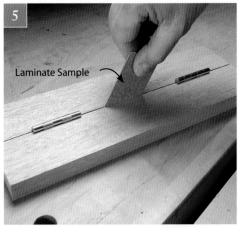

5

Laminate Sample

Test the mortise depth by mounting hinges on scrap stock. The gap should equal the thickness of laminate. If the gap is too wide, the mortises aren't deep enough. Widen a gap that's narrow by jointing the door stile.

6

Mortising Bit

Laminate Trimmer

Rout mortises in the door stile. Locate the mortise at least one hinge length from the top. Because of its small size, a laminate trimmer works great for this delicate job.

7

Transfer the mortise locations from the door to the face frame using a straightedge. The door's snug top-to-bottom fit holds it in position.

8

Mortising Jig

Rout mortises in the face-frame stiles using the mortising jig. You'll need a laminate trimmer for this job, because the mortises are so close to the corner.

parts should have slightly wider gaps, because they'll exhibit greater seasonal movement.

Rout mortises in the door first (Photo 6). Make sure they go in the correct stile! It's easiest to rout hinge mortises all the way through. If you want to rout half-blind mortises, to shoulder the hinge leaves along their length, simply modify your mortising

jig by moving the fill block forward to meet the hinge leaf. This modification eliminates the need for the hinge projection guide, but it requires squaring the mortise corners by hand after routing.

No hard and fast rule exists for locating the hinges on the door. One method is to align the hinge with the door's rails.

However, this doesn't work if the top and bottom rails are distinctly different widths. Another method is to divide the door's length by six or seven and center the hinges one unit from the ends. Use your eye and trust your gut.

Carefully transfer the mortise locations to the face frame (Photo 7). Your marks have to be perfectly located, because the hinges fit the mortises so precisely. Use the door's top-to-bottom friction fit to hold it in position, and make sure the door's hinge stile is flush with the face frame's stile.

Rout mortises in the face frame (Photo 8). If you don't have a laminate trimmer, your options are to chop these mortises by hand or to change your entire procedure and rout these mortises first, before you assemble the face frame.

Mount the Hinges and Create Even Margins

After mounting the hinges on the face frame, temporarily install the door by pressing the mortises onto the mounted hinges' loose leaves. Then mark the door's ends and latch stile for trimming (Photo 9).

Remove the door, clamp on a straight board and rout the ends to final length using a flush-trim bit with two bearings (Photos 10 and 11). Clamp the board so its straight edge barely covers the line; the line indicates the laminate sample's thickness and the goal is to remove exactly that thickness.

Mark the door's final size, using a laminate sample to establish uniform gaps. Slightly recess the door in the opening, using the hinges and the top-to-bottom friction fit to hold it in position. Mark with a mechanical pencil, so there's no gap between the laminate and the line.

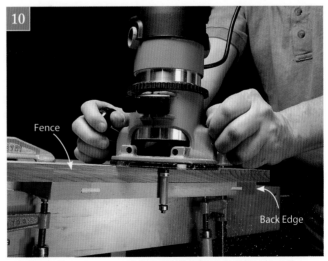

Fence

Back Edge

Rout the door to final length. Use a fence and a flush-trim bit with top- and bottom-mounted bearings to avoid blowing out the back edge. First, rout halfway using the top bearing.

If you build during the summer's high humidity when your lumber is at its widest seasonal dimension, a one-laminate-sample gap between the door's latch stile and the face frame is sufficient. But if you build during the winter, it's wise to provide extra room for the door's seasonal movement (Photo 12).

Flip the door over, adjust the bit to use the bottom bearing, and finish routing.

Allow for seasonal movement between the door's latch stile and the frame. Make the gap wider if you build during the winter, when the humidity in your heated shop is probably significantly lower than during the summer months.

No-Mortise Hinge Options

If mortising hinges isn't your idea of woodworking fun, consider one of these two options for mounting inset doors.

Euro-style hinges only require drilling holes for hinge cups and mounting screws. They also have the advantage of adjustability: Once the door is installed, you can easily move it up or down, side to side and in or out—whatever it takes to even up the margins. These hinges take up a lot of space inside the cabinet, though, and some versions only swing open to 95 degrees.

No-mortise hinges are quite simple to install and they leave an acceptably narrow gap. Some no-mortise hinges have elongated slots for adjustability. Still, the door must be carefully fitted to the opening and the hinge locations have to be carefully laid out. It's a good idea to use a projection guide, like the one shown in Photo 4, to ensure that the door and frame faces will be flush. No-mortise hinges are available in a variety of finishes, including polished and satin brass, but they're often made of plated steel instead of solid brass.

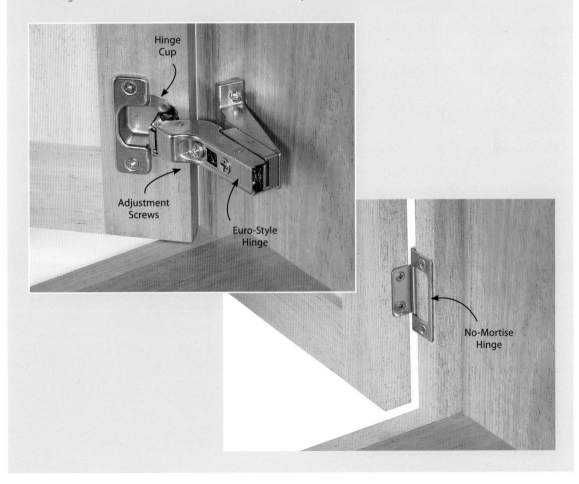

Hinge
Cup

Adjustment
Screws

Euro-Style
Hinge

No-Mortise
Hinge

by TIM JOHNSON

Buying Euro Hinges

CONFUSED BY ALL THE VARIATIONS? HERE'S HOW TO FIND THE HINGES YOU NEED

Euro hinges have revolutionized the way American cabinet shops mount cabinet doors. Originally developed as part of the European frameless cabinetmaking system, Euro hinges work equally well in traditional face-frame cabinets. Also called concealed or cup hinges, these high-tech marvels offer several advantages over traditional hinges.

They're really easy to install. You simply drill holes and pop the hinges and mounting plates into place. Cabinet shops use sophisticated boring machines for production work, but all you really need is a drill press, a 1-3/8-in. flat-bottom boring bit, and a 3/32-in. twist bit.

They make doors mountable in seconds. You just snap Euro hinges into place. Removal's a snap, too.

You can dial in a perfect fit. Euro hinges have adjustment screws that allow you to move the doors up or down, side to side, and front to back after they've been installed.

There's a Euro hinge for almost every door: Thick doors, bi-fold doors, glass doors, doors with narrow stiles or profiled edges. Self-closing hinges are most common, but free-swinging versions are also available.

They don't show. Euro hinges mount behind the doors and inside the cabinet, so they're hidden when the doors are closed.

They're cost-effective. Euro hinges cost more than traditional hinges, but they make installation go a lot faster. Some pro shops charge per door to install traditional hinges.

If Euro hinges have a drawback, it's that there are so many variations it's hard to figure out which ones are right for your project.

Catalogs and Web sites commonly present diagrams and charts to help you choose. Unfortunately, they're almost always loaded with dimensions, unfamiliar terms and installation details that just make things worse. The fact is, you don't have to know a lot about Euro hinges to choose the right ones.

Euro Hinge Basics

Euro hinges vary widely in appearance, but they all share the same basic two-part design and they're all installed the same way. The best Euro hinges are loaded with user-friendly features.

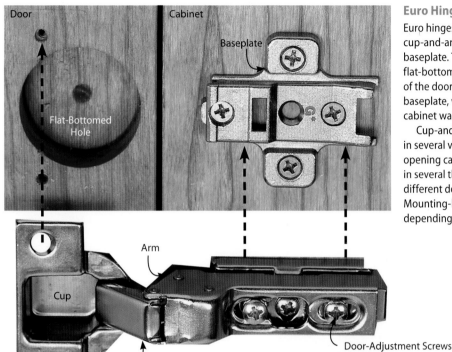

Door

Cabinet

Baseplate

Flat-Bottomed Hole

Arm

Cup

Hinge

Door-Adjustment Screws

Euro Hinge Anatomy

Euro hinges have two parts: a hinged cup-and-arm mechanism and a baseplate. The cup mounts in a flat-bottomed hole drilled in back of the door. The arm locks onto the baseplate, which is fastened to the cabinet wall or face frame.

Cup-and-arm mechanisms come in several variations for different opening capacities. Baseplates come in several thicknesses, to work with different door and cabinet styles. Mounting-hole locations also vary, depending on the application.

Must-Have Features

Snap-on attachment. Spring-lock hinges snap on and off the baseplate with finger pressure. Avoid hinges that clamp to the baseplate with a screw. They can work loose, leaving you with floppy doors.

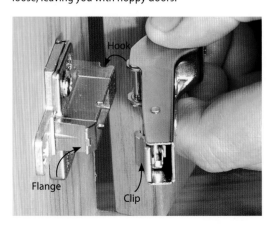

Hook

Flange

Clip

Baseplate

Vertical-Adjustment Screw

Mounting Screw

Simple vertical adjustment. The best hinges allow you to adjust the doors up and down without loosening the mounting screws. These hinges are easy to spot because their baseplates won't have elongated mounting screw holes. Some hinges employ two-part adjustable baseplates (see photo, left). Others locate all three door-adjustment screws on the hinge arm.

Screw-on fastening. Baseplates that mount with regular flat head screws are most economical. All the other fastening variations, like Euro screws and expanding dowels, are aimed at pros. Some require special machinery to install.

Find the Right Hinges

Knowing where you want to use Euro hinges and what you want them to do is most important. Answering 3 simple questions allows you to cut through all the choices and zero in on the right hinge and baseplate combination.

1. What Style Are Your Cabinets?

Face-frame cabinets have frames glued to the front of the cabinet box. This frame makes the cabinet rigid, but it reduces the size of the opening.

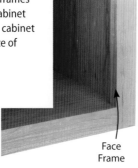

Face Frame

Frameless cabinets are completely open, bordered only by the edges of the cabinet box. The glued-in back makes the cabinet rigid.

2. What Style Are Your Doors?

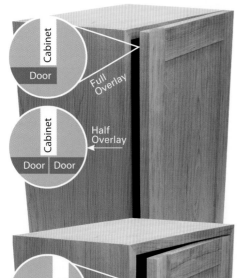

Full Overlay

Half Overlay

Inset

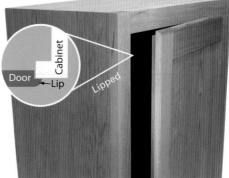

Lip

Lipped

Overlay doors mount in front of the cabinet or face frame. Doors with full-overlay hinges cover the 3/4-in.-wide edge of the frameless cabinet side. Doors with half-overlay hinges cover half of the 3/4-in.-wide edge. You can mount doors on both sides of a single 3/4-in.-wide partition by using half-overlay hinges.

Sometimes, overlay amounts are listed incrementally, ranging from 1/4 in. up to 1-3/8 in. This use of two types of terminology can be confusing: A half-overlay hinge, for example, is not the same as a hinge with a 1/2-in. overlay.

Inset doors mount inside the cabinet or face frame, flush with the front.

Lipped doors fit halfway inside the opening, because the back edge is rabbeted. When the door is closed, the lip covers the opening. Typically, lipped doors are mounted on face-frame cabinets with partially concealed hinges. Few Euro hinges are compatible with lipped doors.

3. How Far Do You Want the Door to Open?

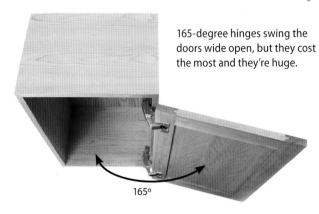

165-degree hinges swing the doors wide open, but they cost the most and they're huge.

165°

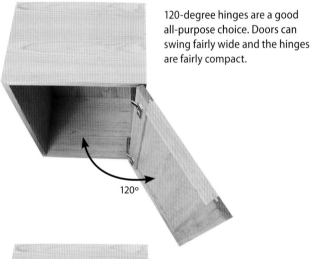

120-degree hinges are a good all-purpose choice. Doors can swing fairly wide and the hinges are fairly compact.

120°

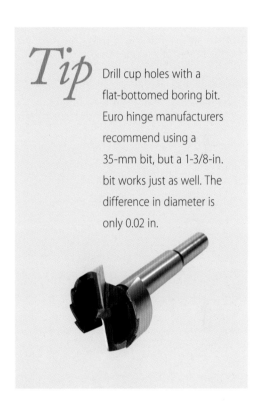

Tip Drill cup holes with a flat-bottomed boring bit. Euro hinge manufacturers recommend using a 35-mm bit, but a 1-3/8-in. bit works just as well. The difference in diameter is only 0.02 in.

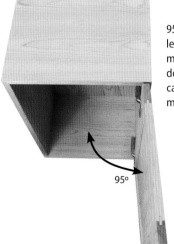

95-degree hinges take up the least cabinet space and are the most economical. However, doors that open only 95 degrees can get in the way when they're mounted on base cabinets.

95°

More Tips for Buying and Using Euro Hinges

High Tech for Traditional Style

Manufacturers have recently introduced
Euro hinges for face-frame cabinets with
inset doors. These hinges represent the
ultimate merging of Euro design and
traditional appearance. Now you can outfit
a classic Shaker-style cupboard or Arts and
Crafts bookcase with high-tech hinges.

Zero-Protrusion
Hinge

Clearance for Pull-Out Shelves

Doors mounted on standard
Euro hinges interfere with
pull-out shelves, because the
doors swing inward as they
open. Cabinets with pull-
out shelves require doors
with special zero-protrusion
hinges. Zero-protrusion
hinges keep the doors from
protruding into the cabinet
opening, so the doors aren't
in the way of the shelves.

Use Three Hinges for Big Doors

Any door taller than 40 in. or wider than 24 in. requires three or more Euro hinges. Suppliers have charts to determine the exact number you'll need.

RAMON MORENO

Buy the Package

Some catalogs offer hinges and backplates separately. This gives professional cabinet-shop buyers all the options. But if you don't know Euro hinges inside and out, it's easiest to buy from a supplier who packages the hinges and baseplates together for specific applications, such as a "frameless cabinet, full-overlay door, 120-degree opening."

Use the Right Driver

Euro-hinge adjustment screws have PoziDrive heads. You can use a Phillips screwdriver on these screws, but a PoziDrive screwdriver works so much better that it's worth having if you're installing more than a few Euro hinges.

A PoziDrive screwdriver has tapered flanges between its 90-degree tips.

Flange

Corner tick marks distinguish PosiDrive screws from Phillips screws.

Tick Mark

by JIM GRANDBOIS

European Hinges

GERMAN ENGINEERING RESULTS IN A CLEAN LOOK AND ADJUSTABILITY

Once I discovered the simplicity of hanging doors with European hinges, I was hooked. Unlike butt hinges, European hinges are totally adjustable and very easy to install. With the help of a simple drill press table and a marking jig, you can hang a door in just a few minutes. Sound good? Read on.

Tools Required

Setting up for European hinges is very simple and quite inexpensive. You only need a drill press, a boring bit, and a screwdriver. The drill press is a must for drilling a straight hole. While you could drill the holes by hand, it's riskier. A drill press ensures success.

If you have a lot of doors to hang, I recommend a 35 mm carbide bit, a self-centering drill bit and a magnetic-tipped screw bit. A 35 mm carbide bit

keeps a sharper edge and outlasts steel bits, especially in tougher materials such as MDF. A self-centering drill bit, such as a Vix bit, is great because it centers the screw hole and controls the drilling depth. In addition, the bit's outer housing protects template holes from damage. A magnetic-tipped screw bit holds screws so well it's the next best thing to an extra hand. Finally, consider spending getting a PoziDrive screwdriver for the adjusting screws. It delivers much better control than a standard Phillips screwdriver.

Figure A: Parts of a European Hinge
These sophisticated hinges allow complete adjustment of a door after installation. In addition, doors can be quickly released from the cabinet without removing a single screw! The hinges keep their settings when reattached—a wonderful feature.

Base-Plate

#6 x 5/8" Woodscrew

#6 x1" Woodscrew

Adjusting Screws

Release Tab

Cover Plate

Hinge Arm

Hinge Cup

#6 x 5/8" Woodscrew

If you have only a few hinges to install, you can save some money. Use a 1-3/8-in. Forstner bit or a 35 mm, high-speed steel bit (costs less than half the carbide). A Phillips screwdriver is fine for installing a few screws and adjusting the hinges.

Installation

I always apply finish to the cabinet and doors before I install hinges. For an inset application (as shown in these photos), cut the doors leaving a 1/8-in. gap at the top, bottom, sides and at the center division between two doors.

Just follow Photos 1 through 8. With all the parts ready to go, installation of European hinges is as easy as *eins, zwei, drei*!

Background

European hinges are part of a standardized construction system developed over 50 years ago in Germany. It radically changed cabinetmaking by streamlining production and reducing costs. The resulting European hinge is a beautifully engineered precision product (Fig. A). There's a hinge for nearly every application. I've used Grass brand hinges for years with flawless results. Major brands such as Grass, Blum, and Mepla make a great product that lasts for years. Expect to pay $10 and up per pair.

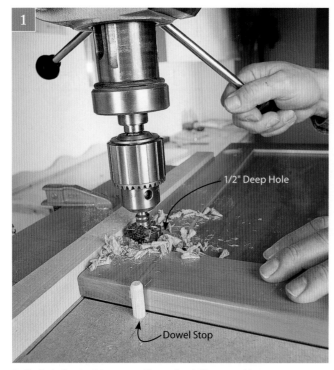

1

1/2" Deep Hole

Dowel Stop

Drill a hole for the hinge cup. Clamp the drill press table in position (Fig. B). Hold the door against the fence, butt it up to the pin and drill the left hinge-cup hole. Pull out the dowel pin and insert it into the right hole of the jig. Then drill the right hinge-cup hole.

Figure B:
Drill Press Table
This easily made jig saves time and helps you achieve consistent results.

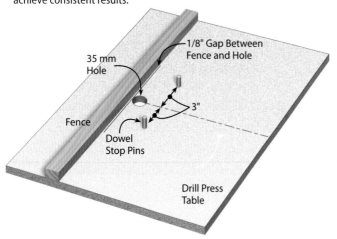

35 mm Hole

1/8" Gap Between Fence and Hole

Fence

3"

Dowel Stop Pins

Drill Press Table

2

Vix Bit

Protective Pad

Screw the hinge to the door. First, insert the hinge and use a square to align the hinge's arm perpendicular to the door. Drill pilot holes into the door using a 7/64-in. Vix bit. (A Vix bit automatically centers the pilot holes at a fixed depth, so you won't accidentally drill through the door.) Install the screws. The soft pad under the door protects the finish.

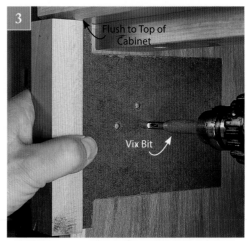

3

Flush to Top of Cabinet

Vix Bit

Drill pilot holes for the baseplate. A simple template automatically locates all four holes (Fig. C). The Vix bit centers the hole, without damaging the template.

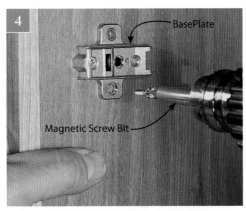

Fasten the baseplate to the cabinet. Install the baseplate with all four screws. A magnetic bit makes it easier to hang on to such a small screw!

Figure C: Baseplate Template for Inset Doors

Instead of measuring and marking the cabinet for each door, make a template to locate the baseplate holes. This one is for inset doors. For overlay doors, the first hole would be about 3/4 in. from the front edge, with the other distances remaining the same.

This template is dimensioned for Grass hinges. However, each application and each brand can have a different drilling pattern, so be sure to read the specs for the hinge you are installing.

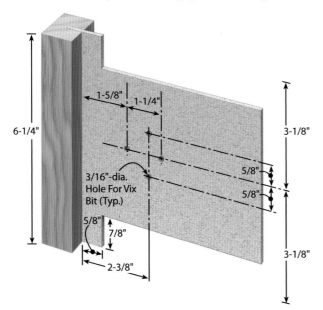

6-1/4"

1-5/8"
1-1/4"

3-1/8"

3/16"-dia. Hole For Vix Bit (Typ.)

5/8"
5/8"

5/8"
7/8"

2-3/8"

3-1/8"

Clip the door onto the baseplates. Attach the upper hinge first. This allows the door to hang so it's easier to handle.

Engage the front of each hinge first. Then push on the back of the hinge arm until it clicks in place.

European hinges make on-site adjustments a snap. Uneven floors and walls can move doors out of line when cabinets are installed. Imagine trying to fix these misaligned doors if they had butt hinges!

Side to Side

Adjust the door left or right with the front screw. This changes the gap between the door and the cabinet side.

This is a direct-action screw, moving the door 1/16 in. per turn. Clockwise rotation decreases the gap between the door and cabinet.

Up and Down

Loosen the middle screw. This adjusts the gap between the door and the top and bottom of the cabinet.

Loosen this screw on both hinges. Move the door to the desired location. Retighten both hinge screws.

In and Out

Loosen the back screw. This adjusts the door so it will be even with the side of the cabinet.

Move the door in or out, then retighten the screw.

Ganz getan (all done)!

Flush With Front

Even Gap

by BRAD HOLDEN

Router-Made Drawer and Door Pulls

IF YOU'RE AFTER A SLEEK, CLEAN LOOK, AN INTEGRATED WOODEN PULL IS A GREAT SOLUTION

Y ou can make integrated pulls yourself using a router table and a few bits. They can be decorative or almost completely hidden. Of the four designs I'll describe for you, two require special bits, but two use ordinary bits that you may already own.

Finger-Pull Door Lip

These doors have a roundover on the back and a decorative cove on the front. The roundover on the back creates just enough room for your fingers to catch hold of the door. This decorative edge treatment around the entire door complements a frame-and-panel style quite nicely. Use European-style hinges and you'll have no visible hardware.

The Bit

Specifically designed for creating pulls, this router bit has no bearing and is quite large with a diameter of 1-3/4 in. Use the bit in a router table and take three or four passes. The door shown is 3/4-in. thick, but this bit will work on doors as thick as 1-1/4 in. Be sure to test the bit on scrap pieces of wood of the same species you're working with and to experiment with different speeds. Some species will chip or splinter at one speed but may work well at a different speed.

Hidden Cove

This hidden pull is made by an ordinary cove bit. It works well on solid wood, fibercore or plywood. On fibercore and plywood, first add a 1/8-in. to 1/4-in. solid-wood edge to the panel's edges and then rout the cove. Some core will be exposed after routing, but it will be hidden after the door is installed.

The Bit

For this cabinet, I used a 1/2-in. cove bit with a bottom bearing. This bit works equally well in a handheld router or a router table. Leave about a 1/4-in. flat lip on the front of the panel.

Dovetail Bevel

This visible decorative pull is made using an ordinary dovetail bit. The entire length of the door's inner edge can be used as a pull. I used a shop-made template as a guide to create a circular design in the middle to complement the cabinet's modern look.

The Setup

Use a router with a guide bushing to follow the template. The template can be made in whatever shape you choose. I chose a circle to add some interest to the simple shape of the cabinet. I used a handheld router so I could easily see when the semicircle was completely cut out. When you're done routing, soften the edges slightly with sandpaper.

The Bit

This 3/4-in.-dia. dovetail bit has a 14-degree angle that leaves an easy-to-grip edge. On these 3/4-in.-thick doors, I set the bit to cut 1/2 in. deep. Any deeper than this would weaken the door's revealed back edge.

Finger Grip

This visible decorative pull is made by a specialty bit. The shape is routed into an applied solid-wood edging. Use stock at least 1-1/2 in. wide. This will result in a nearly 1-in. space for your fingers. You can make it wider if you like, so run a couple of test cuts to figure out how much space is comfortable for you. You don't want to end up scraping your knuckles every time you open the drawer.

The Bit

This bit is designed specifically for creating pulls. The bit has a 3/4-in.-dia. cutter and a 1/2-in. shank. You can use it in a router table or a handheld router. It leaves a smooth, rounded-over front edge, which is easy for your fingers to grip. This bit removes a lot of wood, so make the cut in several light passes, especially as you get closer to your final dimension. It's a real drag to hear a big splinter pop out on the "final" pass. Another option is to first remove the majority of waste with a dado blade on your tablesaw.

by SETH KELLER

Tips for Installing Shelf Supports

THE RIGHT TECHNIQUE MAKES INSTALLATION FAST AND EASY

D rilling shelf-support holes is not difficult, but you only get one chance to get it right. If you make a mistake, you'll get holes that don't line up and shelves that rock or are way out of level. Here are some tips to remove the guesswork from drilling the shelf-support holes and to improve your accuracy. I've also included some tips on which supports are good for glass and other specialty shelving situations.

Mark it up—prevent an Oops! Mark the top of your template. This will help you avoid flipping the template top for bottom and suffering the big mistake of misaligned holes. In addition, drilling shelf-support holes after the cabinet is assembled helps eliminate the risk of drilling holes on the wrong side of a panel.

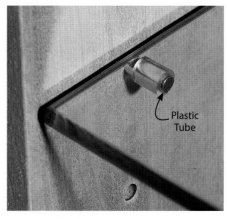

Plastic Tube

Soft Support for Glass Shelves

Straight 5-mm shelf pins with a piece of 1/4-in. outside-diameter (O.D.) aquarium air hose are great for glass shelves. They provide a cushion for the glass, keep it from sliding and reduce the shelf's rattle when the dog runs through the house.

Use a Self-Centering Bit

For perfect alignment every time, use a self-centering bit and a shop-made template. The self-centering bit has an outer sleeve that guides the bit. It also has a built-in depth stop so you don't have to worry about drilling through your cabinet side. The outer guide also prevents the hole in the jig from becoming oversize, which it would if you used an ordinary drill bit.

Shelf Supports for Any Occasion

Some are specialized, others are used mainly for aesthetic purposes and some will save you money if you are using a lot of them. Use pins with a collar when the holes go all the way through a partition. Colored supports blend with the cabinet. Plastic supports are about half the price of metal supports. Supports with locking tabs will keep the shelf in place.

Self-Centering Bit

Black Collared Pin

Chrome Collared Pin

Spoon Pin

1/4" Straight Pin

5-Mm Straight Pin

Pin With Plastic Sleeve

Extra Long Brass Pin

White Support

Brown Support

Clear Support

L-Bracket

L-Bracket For Glass

All Plastic

Support With Lock

L-Bracket
Support

Keep Shelves from Moving

Some L-bracket shelf supports have
a hole in the support that allows you
to screw it to the shelf.

1-1/2"–2"

1"–2"

4"–8"

Practical Spacing for Holes

A practical spacing between shelf supports
is 1 in. to 2 in. between holes and from 4 in.
to 8 in. below the top and above the bottom.
A setback of 1-1/2 in. to 2 in. from the front
and back of the cabinet will give your drill
enough room to maneuver when the back is
on or if there is a face frame.

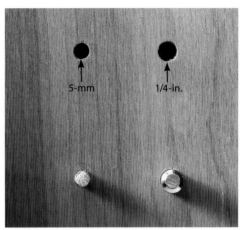

5-mm

1/4-in.

5-mm Holes Look Better

Most shelf supports come in both 1/4-in.
and 5-mm diameters. I prefer the smaller
5-mm hole peg, because it provides a
lighter look and it is less noticeable than
a 1/4-in. hole.

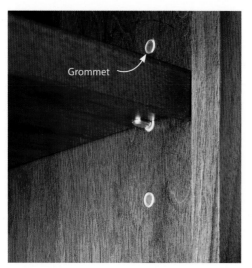

Grommet

Dress Up, Strengthen Holes

These little metal grommets will dress up
your cabinet and, for shelves whose position
is frequently adjusted, will prevent the holes
from wearing. The grommets, available
for both 5-mm and 1/4-in. holes, come in
chrome or brass tone. An oversize drill bit
is required to make holes for the grommets.

Hide Your Supports

Hidden wires are fully concealed when the
shelf is in place. Use a 1/8-in. self-centering
bit and a template to make the holes.
The edge of the shelf needs to be slotted.
This can be done on your tablesaw or with
a slot-cutting router bit. Tip: To simplify
the slotting process, do it before you edge
band. That way you can simply slot the
entire edge and not have to worry about
stopping the slot before you reach the front
of the shelf.

1/8" Hole

Slot

by BRAD HOLDEN

Drawer Slides

NINE MODELS FOR NINE SITUATIONS

Open the drawer of a well-made modern cabinet. How do the slides feel? They should be effortless, smooth and precise. You have more than a dozen types of slides from which to choose. For that perfect glide, the trick is to match the situation and the slide.

Here are nine common kinds of drawers and recommendations for the type of slide to buy for each. As to the specific brand and model, lots of good choices are available.

Dovetailed Drawer

Don't cover beautiful dovetails with a side-mount slide. Use a totally concealed, ball-bearing undermount slide. They're the latest thing for high-end kitchen cabinet drawers. These particular slides are super-smooth and have a self-closing mechanism. Buy the slides before you build the drawers, though. The slides have specific requirements regarding the thickness of the drawer sides and the location of the drawer bottom.

Outdoor Drawer

Exposure to the elements causes a slide to rust and corrode, and there's no easy way to clean it. There is an answer: stainless steel slides rated for outdoor use. They'll hold up well on this patio potting table.

Face-Frame Cabinets

Two simple brackets added to a side-mount, ball-bearing slide make installation a lot easier than building out a cabinet's sides to be flush with the face frame. Fasten the front bracket to the face frame. Clip the slide onto it. Then clip on the rear bracket and attach it to the cabinet's back. If the back is only 1/4 in. thick, apply a mounting block to the back so the bracket's screws can get a solid grip.

Tall Drawer

Stabilize an extra-tall drawer with two pairs of side-mounted slides. With only one pair, this drawer wouldn't open smoothly. These are ball-bearing slides, named after the internal ball bearings on which the components ride. Ball-bearing slides are interchangeable for left and right. That makes installation less confusing, especially when you're using four!

Melamine Drawer

For a white drawer, use a white slide. These particular roller slides are a bottom-mount style, so-called because they wrap around the bottom edge of the drawer side. Melamine drawers are often assembled in the simplest fashion, with a bottom that attaches directly underneath the drawer side. These slides cover that joint and help support the drawer bottom.

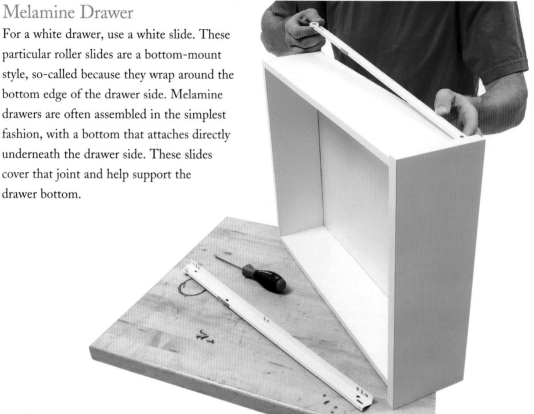

Small Drawer

A small drawer requires an equally small slide. For a piece as nice as this tiny keepsake chest, use a ball-bearing slide. This particular slide doesn't take up much room: One half is housed in the drawer side and the other is only 1/4 in. thick. Unlike other slides, this one doesn't come apart in two pieces. You mount the slide to the cabinet, extend it and add the drawer.

File Drawer

Use an overtravel slide rated to carry a minimum 125-lb. load on a file drawer. An overtravel slide allows the drawer to open about an inch beyond its full depth. This gives you easy access to the rear files. Mounted on an upper drawer, this slide's overtravel would also allow the back of the drawer to open beyond an overhanging desk top.

Shop Drawer

Use roller slides in a dusty shop. The lubrication in a ball-bearing slide would attract sawdust and, in no time, the slide would begin to stick. Roller slides are much easier to keep clean. Simply brush or blow out the sawdust and you're good to go. Tool storage drawers like this one should be capable of carrying a lot of weight. These heavy-duty roller slides can carry a 200-lb. load.

Wide Drawer

A wide drawer is prone to wobble if you use a standard slide. To eliminate racking, use a rack-and-pinion slide. Both sides are connected with a steel rod, so they act in tandem. Installation takes a little extra time, but it's worth it. This Schock-Metall slide is rated for 200 lbs. and can handle a drawer almost 5 ft. wide.

by BRAD HOLDEN

10 Easy Ways to Add Roll-Outs

NINE MODELS FOR NINE SITUATIONS

R oll-out shelving is one of the most popular features of new kitchen cabinets. Mounted on standard drawer slides, these shelves give you easier access to boxes, jars and kitchenware. You can easily add roll-outs to existing cabinets as well. If you do, take three things into account: First, determine whether you must build out the inside of the cabinet so the roll-out and slide clear the door or face frame, including the hinges. Second, choose which kind of drawer slide to use: partial- or full-extension. And third, decide what shape and size to make the roll-out drawer box. These 10 tips cover most of the options— whether you're retrofitting or building new cabinets.

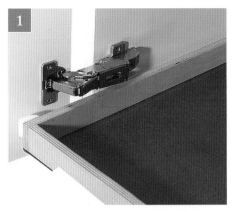

Use Zero-Protrusion Hinges

Zero-protrusion hinges swing the door completely clear of the opening, allowing a roll-out to be pulled out without hitting the door's edge. These hinges let you mount the drawer slides directly to the cabinet sides. Zero-protrusion hinges may be awkward to install in an old cabinet, because they might require new holes.

Attach Slides to a Panel

Mount drawer slides to a new panel so the roll-outs clear the existing hinges or face frame. Then screw the panel to the inside of your cabinet. Make the panel full height to create a finished look on the inside of the cabinet.

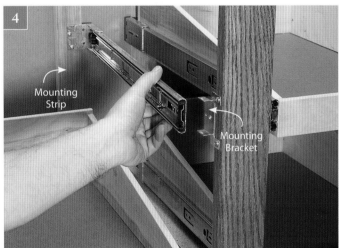

Mount Slides on Plastic Spacers

These spacers provide an easy way to move out your slides so they clear face frames, hinges or doors. They're available in 1/8-in., 3/8-in., 1/2-in., and 3/4-in. heights. After screwing the spacers to the cabinet sides, attach the slides to the spacers with No. 7 wood screws or Pozi-system screws.

Use Mounting Brackets on Face-Frame Cabinets

Mount one bracket on the face frame and the other on the cabinet back. The slides simply snap into place. This cabinet has a 1/8-in. plywood back, which is not thick enough to hold screws. An easy solution is to install 3/4-in. mounting strips on the back using construction adhesive.

Make Adjustable Supports

Make supports from 3-in.-wide boards that are thick enough so the roll-outs clear the face frame and door. Space dadoes at 1-in. intervals. Mount the cabinet part of the slide to a 3/4-in. square strip of wood that is the same length as the cabinet's inside depth. Slip the strips into a set of dadoes and add the roll-out.

Use a Ready-to-Install System

This system is a simple, quick way to add adjustable roll-outs. It uses small blocks called hook dowels that attach to the slide. They fit into square holes spaced at 1-in. intervals in the standards. The mounting strips stand off either 1 or 1-1/4 in. from the cabinet side to clear hinges, face frames or doors.

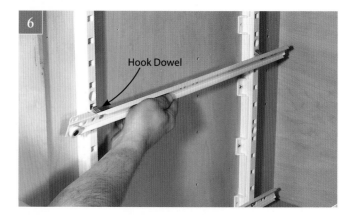

Build Out for Metal Standards

Here's a simple way to install roll-outs in cabinets that have metal shelf standards: Mount your slides to plastic spacer blocks that have shelf clips on their backs. The system is quick and adjustable, but be sure to check for pound rating per roll-out.

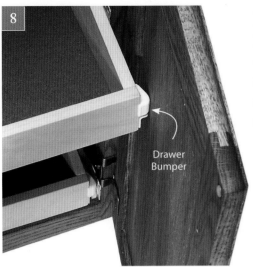

8

Drawer
Bumper

Prevent Door Damage with Bumpers

Install drawer bumpers to prevent slides from scratching a door. These bumpers extend beyond most bottom-mounted epoxy-style slides, but you may need to add a spacer, such as a washer or cardboard shim, behind the bumper to keep a full-extension ball-bearing slide from scratching the door.

9

Full Extension
Slide

Corral Stuff with Tall Backs and Sides

Build your roll-outs with tall backs and sides if they will carry tall or stacked items. Make the front low to keep items easily accessible. Full-extension slides provide easy access to the contents at the roll-out's back. They cost about twice the price of three-quarter-extension, bottom-mounted, epoxy-style slides, though.

10

Extended
Drawer
Front

Hide the Slides

For a refined look, extend roll-out fronts to cover the ends of the slides. Use dadoes to attach an extended front on shallow roll-outs. For taller roll-outs, use biscuits.

by BRAD HOLDEN

Under-Cabinet Lighting

ADD A GLOWING TOUCH TO BEAUTIFUL CABINETS

Want a quick way to improve upper kitchen cabinets? Install lights under them. Under-cabinet lights eliminate shadows in work areas and improve the room's atmosphere. Some may be controlled with a dimmer switch to make your kitchen even more inviting. You can design cabinets to accommodate these lights and wiring or add them after the cabinets have been built and installed.

Four major types of under-cabinet light fixtures are available: fluorescent, halogen, xenon, and light-emitting diode (LED). Some can be dimmed; others cannot. Some emit warm, golden light; others shine a cool light that's closer to daylight. Learning about the features, pros and cons of each type will help you select the best options for your kitchen cabinets.

Features

All four types of under-cabinet lighting are available in easy-to-install fixtures. Often, individual lights plug into power blocks, which connect to a transformer (see photo, bottom). The transformer plugs into a wall socket. On larger units, the transformer is housed in the fixture.

Fluorescent and LED under-cabinet lights cast warm-colored light (left) or cool-colored light (right), depending on the bulbs you select. Halogen and xenon fixtures cast a warm light.

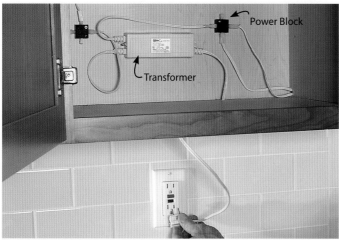

Under-cabinet lighting can be easy to install. Many fixtures plug directly into multiple-outlet power blocks, which in turn plug into a transformer. Plug the transformer into an existing wall socket.

Fixtures can be purchased as individual components or complete kits. Kits include everything you need: transformers, connectors, plugs and power blocks.

Some fixtures can be hardwired if you want to hide wires inside a wall or use a switch mounted in a wall. In this case, you wire the transformer into a junction box, then plug the fixtures into the transformer.

Dimming Capability

Only halogen and xenon lights can be dimmed, a feature I really like. I turn my kitchen lights all the way up when I'm working and dim them for a more relaxing ambience when it's time to eat. There are three switching options: an add-on touch-pad dimmer, a hardwired wall switch or a fixture with a high and low setting. Xenon lights must be hardwired if you wish to dim them. Halogen lights can be hardwired or installed with a touch-pad dimmer. The dimmer can sit on the counter or mount under the cabinet near the lights. It's as easy as plugging the transformer into the dimmer and plugging the dimmer into a wall outlet.

Warm, Cool or Neutral Light

Color temperature, given in degrees Kelvin (K), indicates a light's color appearance. Warm lights below 3,500 K project a yellow or orange appearance. Cool lights above 3,500 K emit a blue or green cast. Fluorescent and LED lights run the spectrum from warm to cool.

Halogen and xenon lights emit a warm cast. Most people prefer lighting that appears warm.

Spot or Strip Lights

All four types of lights are available in small spot or puck lights, or long strip fixtures. Puck lights are more versatile. They can fit into small spaces or can be linked together to cover a large area. Use one puck light every 12 to 18 in.

Energy Efficiency

Fluorescent and LED lights are about five times more efficient than halogen and xenon lights.

Under-Cabinet Lighting Types

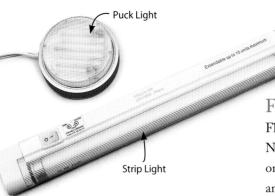

Puck Light

Strip Light

Extendable up to 10 units maximum

Fluorescent

Fluorescent lights have come a long way in recent years. New fixtures don't hum or flicker when they're turned on. Fluorescent lightbulbs are available in warm, cool and daylight color casts. They're efficient and don't produce much heat, making them comfortable to work near. In addition, they won't melt the butter on your counter! A typical fluorescent under-cabinet lightbulb will last 10,000 to 20,000 hours. Along with the familiar strip form, fluorescent lights are also available as compact puck lights. Most fluorescent lights are not dimmable.

Type of Light	Light Output (lumens per watt)	Average bulb life	Color Temperature (degrees Kelvin)	Dimmable
Incandescent (100 watt)	13 lw	1,000 hours	2,750 K	Yes
Fluorescent (48" 28 watt)	82 lw	10,000 to 20,000 hrs.	3,000 to 6,000 K	No
Halogen	19 lw	2,000 to 4,000 hrs.	3,000 K	Yes
Xenon	15 lw	8,000 to 10,000 hrs.	2,700 K	Yes
LED	80 lw	20,000 to 50,000 hrs.	3,200 to 5,500 K	No
Midday sunlight	NA	NA	5,500 K	NA
Candlelight	NA	NA	1,500 K	NA

Halogen

Halogen lights produce crisp, warm white light very similar to what standard incandescent bulbs emit. In fact, halogens are incandescent bulbs with halogen gas inside to prolong the filament's life. Halogens are dimmable, compact and available in pucks or strips. The main drawbacks are that they're not as efficient as LEDs and fluorescents, and they generate a lot of heat. A halogen bulb lasts as long as 4,000 hours. That's the shortest bulb life-span of the four types of fixtures, but much better than a standard incandescent bulb, which lasts from 750 to 2,000 hours.

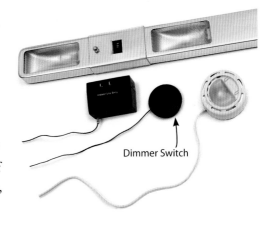

Dimmer Switch

Xenon

Xenon lights are incandescent bulbs that contain xenon gas to extend the filament's life. A xenon bulb produces light similar to that of a standard incandescent, only slightly less yellow in color. And it will last 8,000 to 10,000 hours. Most xenon lights may be dimmed if they're hardwired to a standard dimmer switch. Xenon bulbs are available with two different bases. The more standard xenon bulb has a wedge-shaped base; a bi-pin base is available as a replacement bulb for some halogen fixtures. Xenon lights last longer and generate about 15 percent less heat than halogen lights do.

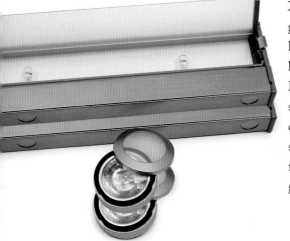

LED

LED lights are available in fixtures that produce either warm or cool white light. They're extremely compact and consume miniscule amounts of energy—a single fixture with three bulbs uses only 3 watts. They generate very little heat and last as long as 50,000 hours. LED lights have two drawbacks. First, they're not dimmable. Second, they're expensive: Expect to pay $100 or more for a high-quality under-cabinet fixture.

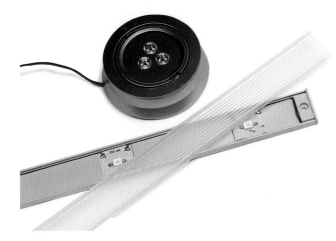

Laminate and Countertops

If your cabinet project involves a kitchen or bathroom, you will likely need a countertop. Plastic laminate is the most commonly available countertop material. When you combine its reasonable cost, low maintenance requirements, and durability, it's easy to understand why it's a great choice for most kitchens and bathrooms. The most common core or substrate material for counter tops is particleboard. Not all particleboards are created equal though. If it's not marked, ask your lumber dealer for advice. Most important is that it has a level, smooth surface. With intermediate woodworking skills, attention to detail, and a few extra tools specific to laminate work, you'll be able to build and install a laminate countertop. Build a small laminate project before you tackle an entire kitchen. Plastic laminate is fairly simple to work with, but just like building with wood, it's best to practice first, measure twice, and cut once—or have a thick wallet.

by DAVID RADTKE

Working with Plastic Laminate

LEARN TO USE THIS DURABLE, VERSATILE MATERIAL IN YOUR HOME AND SHOP

Most woodworkers probably have a natural aversion to working with plastic laminate. After all, we love wood, not plastic! I managed to steer clear of the stuff for years before a bathroom vanity job forced me into it. I was surprised to find it wasn't so bad! I'd been missing out on a great product that has a thousand uses beyond the durable, easy-to-clean countertops found in kitchens and baths.

Think Outside the Countertop

Plastic laminate has a hundred uses beyond the kitchen countertop. Around the shop, it makes an ideal wear surface for jigs, fences, extension tables, assembly benches—anywhere a tough, easy-to-clean, low-friction surface is needed.

Unlike wood, plastic laminate requires no clamping, sanding, staining, painting or varnishing. After machining, you're left with a perfectly smooth, colorful and durable surface that's ready to use.

Plastic laminate not only creates a durable surface, it also adds significant strength. For example, a particleboard shelf with a laminate top, bottom and edge can hold three times the weight of a raw, uncovered particleboard shelf.

Plastic laminate can also liven up your projects with bold colors. Whether it's multicolored shelving or a dark green top on a walnut computer desk, plastic laminates offer a broad palette of colors. You can even find some pretty good imitations of leather and metal.

So, if you've shied away from working with plastic laminate, it's time to get familiar with this durable and versatile material.

In this article we'll walk you through making a basic countertop with radiused corners. We'll also show you how to make a countertop with a wood edge. Laminate requires a few specialty tools and some practice, but once you master the skills, you may find yourself choosing plastic laminate for countertops, shop fixtures, doors—all sorts of projects!

EDITOR: DAVE MUNKITTRICK • ART DIRECTION: VERN JOHNSON AND BILL FABER • PHOTOGRAPHY: BILL ZUEHLKE AND RAMON MORENO

Must-Have and Nice-to-Have Tools

Must-Have Tools and Materials

Contact Cement

Contact cement is the best adhesive for laminate work. It creates an instant bond and eliminates the need for clamps. Contact cement is available in both solvent-based and water-based formulas. The fumes from solvent-based contact cement are toxic and flammable. For that reason, we recommend water-based contact cement. It's much safer to use and cleans up easily with soap and water. The only drawback to water-based contact cement is its longer drying time, especially in humid conditions. Follow the recommended safety guidelines on the back of the container.

Cement Applicators

All you need here is a disposable brush and a 9-in. roller. Look for roller covers specially designed for spreading adhesives. If you choose to use solvent-based contact cement, don't use foam applicators. The solvents eat them up.

A Router

Any router will do, but smaller is better. Bigger routers have larger bases that tend to get in the way. Laminate trimmers are very small routers made just for this type of work. If you do a lot of laminate work, they are worth the extra cash because they're so easy to handle.

Laminate-Trimming Bits

You'll need two carbide router bits to cut plastic laminate; a flush-trim bit and a bevel-trim bit. The flush-trim bit cuts the laminate flush with the particleboard base (called a substrate). The bevel-trim bit is used to ease the edge where laminate meets laminate at a 90-degree angle (for example, the spot where the edge and top of a countertop meet).

Flush-Trim Bit

Bevel-Trim Bit

Heat Gun

To bend laminate around a radius, you'll need a heat gun, which softens the laminate so it won't break as it's bent. We'll show you how to do this later.

Nice-to-Have Tools

Scoring Cutter

If cutting a flimsy piece of laminate with power tools makes you nervous, this may be the tool for you. It's a carbide-tipped hand tool that scores the surface of the laminate. After scoring, the laminate will break along the score line. It's similar to cutting drywall or glass.

Single-Cut Mill/Bastard File

This tool is used to ease any sharp edges or straighten any irregularities after trimming. Look for one labeled "mill/bastard type" on the package.

J-Roller

This tool is used to roll the surface of the laminate to ensure a complete adhesive bond to the substrate. In a pinch, you can substitute a 2x4 block with a rag wrapped around it.

What Is Plastic Laminate?

Very simply put, plastic laminate is made with layers of paper and resins pressed together under high temperatures and pressure to form a sheet about 1/16-in. thick. The top layer of paper gives the laminate its color.

Don't mistake melamine for plastic laminate. Melamine is really only the single colored layer pressed onto one or two sides of particleboard. Because the colored layer is so thin, melamine does not wear as well as laminate. Also, it's not available in as wide a selection of colors, textures or patterns.

Many home centers carry plastic laminate, but the choices are limited, and the sheets are usually 4x8 and smaller. However, you can special order sheets up to 5 ft. x 12 ft., in a wide array of colors and textures.

Choosing a Substrate

Plastic laminate is so thin, the surface underneath it (the substrate) must be sturdy and smooth. Because it's relatively cheap, the most popular choice for a substrate is 3/4-in. high-density particleboard. Medium-density fiberboard (MDF) works equally well but will cost you about 30-percent more. All of these substrates are sold at home centers in 4x8 sheets.

 Tip Hang on to your leftovers. Scraps of plastic laminate make great shim stock for setting an even gap around drawers and doors.

Making a Basic Countertop

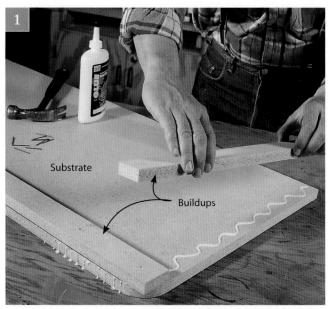

Glue and clamp the buildups to the bottom of the substrate to give the countertop a thicker, more substantial appearance. Use nails to pin the buildups in place so they won't shift around under clamp pressure.

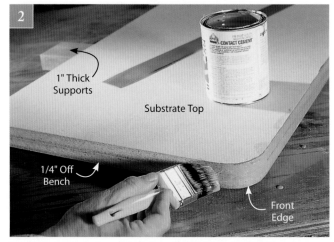

Brush contact cement on the edges. Particleboard edges are porous and may require two coats (let the first coat dry about 30 minutes). Brush contact cement on the back of the laminate strip when you apply the second coat to the edge. Use supports to hold the substrate off the bench.

3 Ways to Cut Plastic Laminate

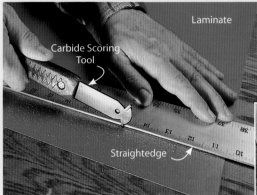

Cut the laminate with a carbide-tipped scoring tool. Make at least four firm passes to score deep enough for a clean break. Pull up gradually from one end of the score to the other (inset photo).

Laminate

Carbide Scoring Tool

Straightedge

Cut the laminate with a circular saw. Set the blade 1/4-in. deep and hold the laminate up off your bench with 2x4s, as shown. Use a high-tooth-count, carbide blade in your saw. Secure the laminate face down on the 2x4s with tape.

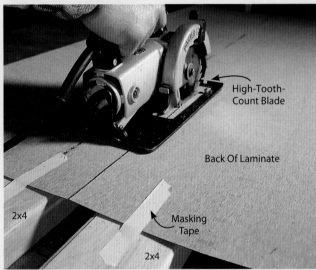

High-Tooth-Count Blade

Back Of Laminate

2x4

Masking Tape

2x4

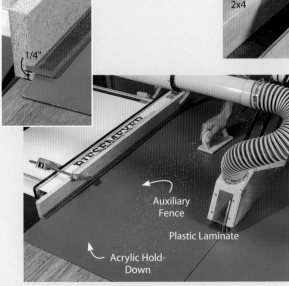

1/4"

Auxiliary Fence

Plastic Laminate

Acrylic Hold-Down

Cut laminate with a subfence on your tablesaw. The simple subfence shown here fits tight to the top of your tablesaw so the laminate can't sneak under the fence and get jammed.

A narrow strip of acrylic holds the laminate down on the table while letting you see where the laminate contacts the fence.

Build the Substrate

Make sure the substrate is perfectly clean, flat and free of blemishes, because they're sure to show through the laminate. Cut your top to size on the tablesaw. Countertops typically have a built-up edge to give them a more substantial look. Cut 2-in.-wide strips of particleboard for front-edge buildups. Glue and nail (or clamp) the strips to the outside edges for a full 1-1/2-in.-thick nosing (Photo 1). Use a portable jigsaw to cut a 2-in. radius on the outside corners. Then sand the edges and radiused corners perfectly even.

Cut the Plastic Laminate to Size

Once your substrate is built, you're ready to cut the laminate sheet to size. Full sheets of laminate are flimsy and hard to handle. If you're working alone, we recommend cutting the sheets down to manageable size using a scoring tool or a circular saw (photo, page 155). You can also cut laminate on your tablesaw using a simple hold-down jig (photo, page 155). Cut the laminate 1/2-in. larger in width and length than the substrate dimensions. Cut the large surface piece first, then the thin strip for the vertical edge.

Now you're ready to cement the laminate to the substrate. Remember, contact cement works differently than other adhesives. After coating both surfaces to be bonded you let the cement dry before you put them together. Once dry, the two surfaces will bond instantly on contact, and there's no turning back. You can't reposition the piece. Weird stuff, but it really is the best adhesive for laminate work.

Apply the Laminate Edge

For countertops, always do the vertical surfaces first and the top or horizontal surface, last. That way the horizontal top overlaps and protects the vertical edge from chipping when you drag heavy appliances or dishes off the countertop. For vertical surfaces like doors, it's just the opposite; horizontal first and vertical, or edges, last.

Position the substrate onto a couple pieces of 1-in. scrap so the bottom of the built-up edge is 1/4 in. off your bench (Photo 2). This will accommodate the 1/4-in. overhang of the laminate piece and allow you to use your bench as a guide for getting the strip placed evenly on the substrate.

 Tip If your trimming bit gets clogged with contact cement, you'll need to clean it. Turn off the router, remove the bit and soak it in mineral spirits. Use an old toothbrush to remove the cement.

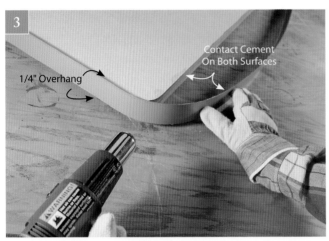

3

1/4" Overhang

Contact Cement
On Both Surfaces

Use a heat gun on curves to soften the laminate. Press the laminate onto the substrate with a gloved hand.

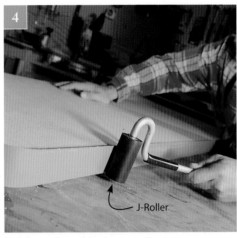

4

J-Roller

Roll the surface of the laminate firmly to ensure a good bond to the substrate.

5

Laminate
Flush-Trim Bit

Trim the top and bottom edge of the laminate strip flush to the substrate. Use a laminate flush-trim bit for this job. Be careful not to tip the router as you cut.

6

Mill/Bastard File

Smooth any irregularities left after routing with a file or sanding block. Be careful not to round over the edge. File only in the direction that pushes the laminate into the substrate, not away from it.

Apply contact cement to the edge of the substrate and the back of the laminate strip.

Let both surfaces dry to the touch. Depending on the humidity, this could take as long as an hour or as little as 15 minutes. Touch it with your fingertips to test for dryness. The cement should not stick to your finger. Keep the bottom edge of the laminate strip in contact with your benchtop to keep the strip parallel to the substrate. Start at one end and carefully press the laminate strip to the edge of the substrate. Don't forget about those radiused corners! When you're a couple inches away from the radius, grab your heat gun and heat the laminate strip a few inches on both sides of the radius (Photo 3). Gently bend the laminate strip around the curve and work your way to the end. To ensure a complete bond, apply pressure along the entire edge with a J-roller (Photo 4).

Flush-Trim the Overhang

Now you can trim the edges flush with the substrate. Hang the edge of the workpiece over your work surface to allow room for the router base. Clamp the countertop in place. Install your laminate flush-trim bit in your router. Trim the top and bottom edges (Photo 5).

Use a file or sanding block with 120-grit paper to make sure the top and bottom edges are perfectly flat (Photo 6).

Oops!

Oh, great! I got a little too close to the overhanging edge when I rolled out the top. The unsupported laminate cracked all the way back to the substrate. Unfortunately, this is impossible to repair. You must cut new laminate. Fortunately, you can remove the broken laminate and use the substrate again. Contact cement is reversible. Just squirt or brush some mineral spirits into the joint as you peel off the broken laminate (see photo below). The mineral spirits will break the bond. Remember, you must recoat the substrate with a fresh coat of contact cement to create a new bond.

Roll contact cement on the substrate and the back of the plastic laminate. Let it dry on both surfaces before assembly.

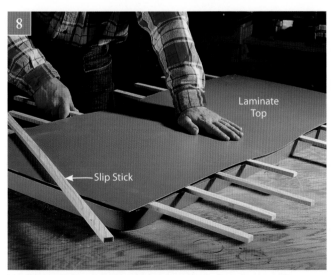

Use "slip sticks" to separate the laminate from the substrate. Align the laminate top with the substrate, keeping a 1/4-in. overhang on all sides. Remember: You won't be able to move the laminate once it touches the substrate. Start in the middle and pull out the slip sticks one by one, pushing the laminate onto the substrate as you go.

Apply the Laminate Top

Double- and triple-check that the substrate surface is completely clean! Even the tiniest wood chip or bit of dust will create a bump in the smooth laminate surface. Coat the top of the substrate and back of the laminate with contact cement using a lint-free paint roller (Photo 7). Cover it generously but keep it from oozing onto the edge face. Wipe off any overflow with a damp rag. When the cement is dry, place clean, splinter-free slip sticks, about 4 to 5 in. apart, onto the substrate top (Photo 8). Slip sticks can be 1/2-in. dowels or square pieces of wood. The slip sticks keep the two cement-coated surfaces from touching until you get the top positioned precisely. Flip the laminate onto the slip sticks so you've got an even 1/4-in. overhang all around.

Don't get over-anxious with this step. Starting in the middle, gently pull out the slip sticks and press the laminate onto the substrate. Work your way to one end and come back to the middle and work your way to the other end.

Use a J-roller over the entire surface to ensure a good bond. Be careful with the roller near the edges. Getting too close to the overhanging edge could snap the laminate (see Oops!, opposite). If you don't have a roller, just wrap a cotton rag around a 2x4 and push the edge of the covered 2x4 firmly over the entire area.

Trim the Laminate Top

Use a little mineral spirits on a rag and rub any excess contact cement from the face of the laminated edge until it's perfectly clean. To protect the vertical edge from burn marks as you trim, cover the front edge with masking tape. Keep the tape a hair below the top edge (Photo 9).

Next, flush-trim the laminate with your router. Note: Be sure there are no burrs or loose screws on your router base that could scratch the laminate. Use a sanding block with some 220-grit paper to remove burrs. Trim the top, letting the bearing ride along the taped edge (Photo 9). Move the router from left to right, keeping the base flat on the top.

Ease the sharp top edge where the laminate meets with a bevel-trim bit (Photo 10). Install the bevel-trim bit in your router so only 3/16 in. or less of the cutting edge is exposed. Bevel the top edge only. Now step back and admire your work.

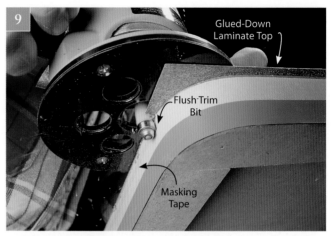

Trim the laminate flush with the substrate all the way around the top. Masking tape protects the laminate from scorching should the bearing get clogged with contact cement and seize up.

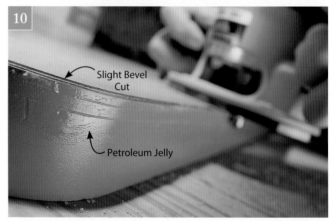

Use a bevel-trim bit to ease the sharp edge where the two laminate pieces overlap. A thin coat of lubricant, such as petroleum jelly, protects the finished edge from scarring.

Making a Wood-Edged Top

A wood-edged countertop not only looks great, but it's easy to make, holds up better than laminate edges and you can choose from a variety of edge profiles.

Prepare the substrate as you would for a laminate-edged top. Cut and glue 3/4-in. x 1-1/2-in.-hardwood edge banding onto the built-up substrate. Mitered corners look best. Round the sharp outside corners, sand the wood edge flush with the substrate (top photo), and apply the laminate top. Flush-trim the laminate to the substrate. Then, choose a router bit profile to finish off the edge. I like a simple bevel cut (bottom photo), but you could choose any number of profiles.

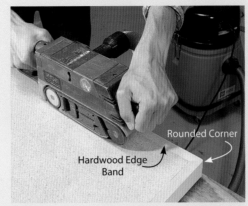

Sand the wood edge flush with the top of the substrate. Round over the mitered corners with a router before applying the laminate.

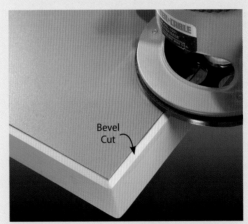

Use a chamfer bit to shape the top edge of the countertop. A 25- to 30-degree bevel looks best. You can choose any number of router-bit profiles as an edge treatment on a wood-edged countertop.

by DAVE MUNKITTRICK

Working with Melamine

IT'S DIRT CHEAP, IT'S PRACTICAL, AND BEST OF ALL, THERE'S NO SANDING AND FINISHING!

Melamine is the professional cabinetmaker's best friend. Build a cabinet with it and you have a complete, durable interior that requires no sanding (yes!) and no finishing (oh, yeah!). Pros often build whole kitchens out of melamine and then dress the boxes with plywood end panels and solid-wood fronts. The bright melamine cabinet interiors are easy to search, stain resistant and tough as nails. Entertainment centers and home office, laundry-room or mudroom cabinets are also made with melamine. Most home centers carry melamine shelving with the edge banding already on. Just buy or make shelf supports and you're in business.

Melamine has found a home in many a woodshop. The durable, slick surface is perfect for jigs, fences, outfeed tables and router tables. I use it in my shop as an assembly table cover. Glue drips pop right off and the slick surface makes it easy to slide around heavy assemblies. It's not as durable as plastic laminate for high-wear surfaces such as countertops and desktops, but it's plenty tough for shop use.

Still not sold on melamine? How about saving money? It's about half the cost of birch plywood. Not only that, but you get better yield from a sheet of melamine than from veneer sheet stock. That's because you don't have to worry about grain direction. Better yield at a lower cost—you save both ways.

Here are some tips on how to make this staple material of the modern cabinetmaker work perfectly for you!

ART DIRECTION: SARA KOEHLER • PHOTOGRAPHY: RAMON MORENO

Go Beyond Basic White

White melamine is by far the most common, but basic colors, like black, almond and wood grain, can be special-ordered from most home centers or lumberyards that carry the white. Melamine comes in a wide range of thicknesses. Home centers not only carry 3/4-in. and 5/8-in. sheets for cabinet construction and shelving, but they often have 1/2-in. for drawer parts and 1/4-in. stock for backs and drawer bottoms.

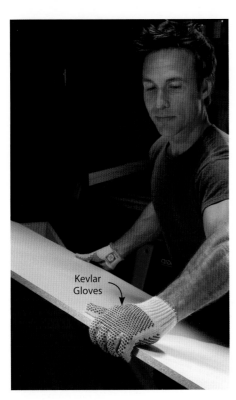

Kevlar Gloves

Wear Gloves!

Gloves are a must when handling large sheets of melamine. We recommend a pair of Kevlar® gloves. Kevlar is designed to protect the user from slicing cuts. Surprisingly, they're inexpensive and the rubber dots or stripes help you get a grip on the slippery melamine surface.

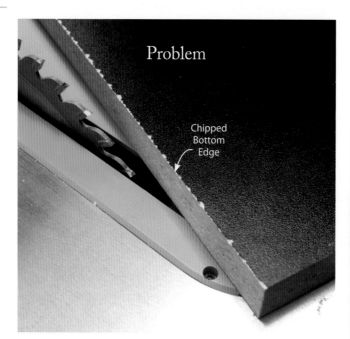

Problem

Chipped
Bottom
Edge

Stop the Chip-Out Monster

Chip-out on the bottom edge is a common problem when
you use a general-purpose blade to cut melamine. Sometimes
one rough edge doesn't matter, but when you need a perfectly
clean edge on both sides, you have a couple options. The first
is to make a 1/16-in.-deep scoring cut on the bottom of the
piece (see photo, right). Turn the saw off and crank up
the blade to finish the cut. The result is a perfectly clean
cut on both surfaces.

Solution 1

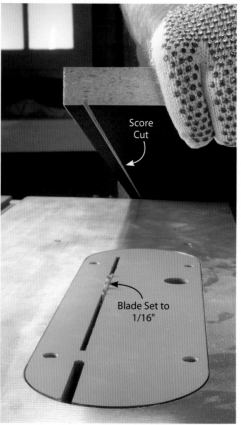

Score
Cut

Blade Set to
1/16"

Solution 2

The second solution is a laminate-cutting
blade (right), which gives you perfectly
clean edges on both sides, without a scoring
cut. If you cut a lot of melamine, these
blades are well worth the investment.

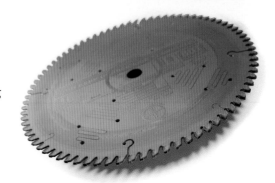

Use Your Router to Drill Holes

Drilling for adjustable shelves can be a problem in melamine. A sharp brad-point bit will make a clean hole, but the melamine is hard on the cutting edges and a typical bit will quickly dull. Production shops use special carbide-tipped bits that are expensive and hard to find.

For the weekend builder, the best way to drill holes in melamine is to use a router. A simple jig and a plunge router with a 5/8-in. guide bushing is the way to go. Use a 1/4-in. carbide down-spiral bit for flawless holes.

The jig is simply a piece of 1/2-in. plywood with a series of 5/8-in. holes spaced at 2-in. intervals. Clamp the jig flush with the case side, set the bushing in the first hole and plunge. Repeat the process until all the holes are drilled.

5/8" Holes

Drilling Jig

A Tongue Makes Dado Joints Easier

Routers are great for cutting dadoes in melamine, because it assures a chip-free cut. Unfortunately, melamine is about 1/128-in. over 3/4-in. As a result, if you try to use a 3/4-in. router bit to cut a dado, it'll be slightly undersized—not a pretty picture come assembly time. You can get around this by making a 1/2-in. dado and creating a 1/2-in. tongue on the ends of the shelf with a rabbeting bit.

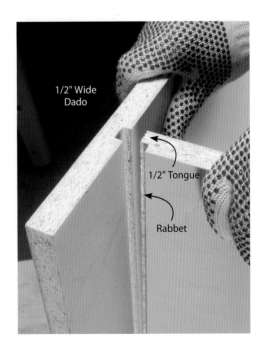

1/2" Wide Dado

1/2" Tongue

Rabbet

Reinforce Joints with Melamine Glue

Typical wood glue won't bond at all to melamine's slick surface. That leaves you with a weakened glue joint where melamine meets particleboard. Fortunately, you can buy specialized glue that will bond melamine to a porous surface like particleboard. This is especially critical on more delicate joints, for instance, those used to construct a drawer.

Throw Away Your Iron

Melamine needs to be edged for a finished look. You can use iron-on edging, but self-stick edging is faster, easier and incredibly strong. Just peel, stick, and give it a pass with a wood block or roller to push the adhesive into the particleboard. Maximum strength is obtained in a week. One swipe with a double-sided edge trimmer cuts the tape flush.

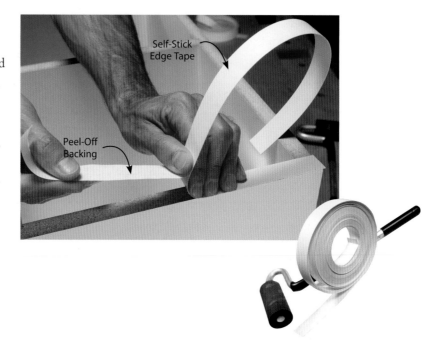

Self-Stick
Edge Tape

Peel-Off
Backing

Cover Unsightly Holes

The easiest way to cover exposed screw heads is with Fast Cap self-stick caps. These discs come in typical melamine colors and they're a cinch to apply—just peel and stick.

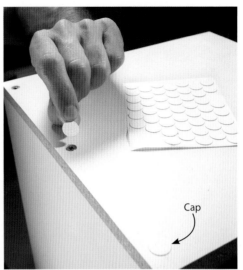

Cap

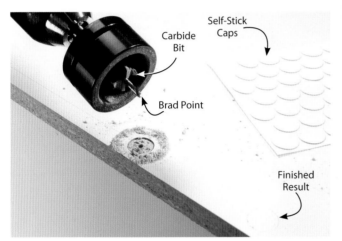

Carbide Bit

Self-Stick Caps

Brad Point

Finished Result

Flush-Fit Caps Appear Invisible

A flush-fit screw cap looks a whole lot better than the surface-applied caps. Plus, they are less prone to getting knocked off. The FlushMount carbide drill bit cuts a shallow 9/16-in.-dia. countersink for the self-stick cap. An adjustable brad-point bit protruding through the center of the carbide bit drills the pilot hole. Both bits can be adjusted for depth of cut. Just drill, screw and cover. The caps are almost invisible. The same system can be used on wood-veneered sheet stock.

Repair

Gouge

Repair, Don't Despair

Small nicks and gouges are easy to fix using SeamFil. It works just like wood filler but it's designed for plastic. Just work a little into the wound and scrape it flush using a putty knife. After the filler dries, use a utility razor to remove any excess. It makes a quick, easy repair that's only noticeable at close range.

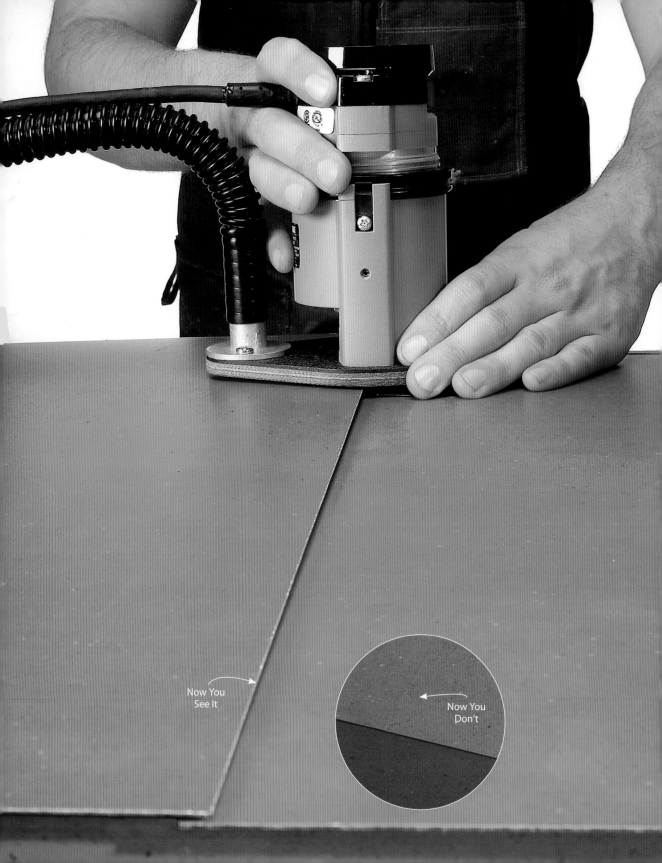

Now You
See It

Now You
Don't

by BRAD HOLDEN

Perfect Butt Joints in Laminate

AN UNDERSCRIBE ROUTER ATTACHMENT GUARANTEES SUCCESS

EDITOR: MANDY JOHNSON • ART DIRECTION: DAVID SIMPSON • PHOTOGRAPHY: JOE GOHMAN • ILLUSTRATION: FRANK ROHRBACH

Long countertops or those that turn corners need butt joints. You can use several methods to make this joint, but the easiest way to get tight-fitting, professional-looking results is with an underscribe attachment on a trim router. The term underscribe refers to the attachment riding under the piece being scribed. The cut is guided by a small lip on the underside of the attachment that follows the straight edge on the bottom piece of laminate (see Fig. A).

1. Start by making a couple of small (approximately 12-in. x 12-in.) test countertops from scraps of the same laminate you will use in your finished project. Using the same kind of laminate is important, because even a small difference in laminate thickness will affect the accuracy and fit of the final joint. Use the test countertops and Steps 2 through 9, to set up the underscribe attachment. Rout an inch or two on one of the test tops, check the fit and adjust the underscribe base as necessary. The base has built-in micro-adjusters, so fine-tuning is simple. When you have

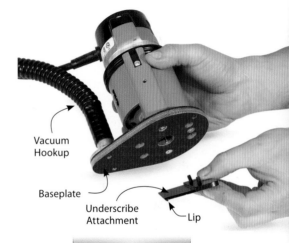

Vacuum Hookup

Baseplate

Underscribe Attachment — Lip

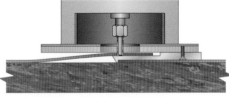

Figure A:
Underscribe Attachment Detail

The underscribe attachment has a lip that rides on the straight edge of the bottom piece of laminate and lifts the edge of the top piece while a 1/8-in. router bit does the cutting.

the perfect fit, run one more test cut using the entire joint on one of the test countertops. You will only get one shot at your project, so now is the time to fine-tune the attachment to perfection.

2. Rout a straight edge on one piece of laminate (Photo 1). You'll end up with a small burr on the bottom edge of the laminate. Remove the burr with a file, so the laminate will glue down completely flat. Mark a straight pencil line along this straight edge. The lip on the underscribe attachment rides on this edge and guides the router through the cut. As a result, this first piece of laminate is called the guide piece. Mark the adjoining edge on the second piece of laminate with a wavy line to show that it has a rough edge (Photo 2).

3. Position the guide piece on the substrate without adhesive and make a pencil line on the substrate along the laminate's straight edge. Next, lay down the second piece, overlapping the guide piece by 1/4 in. to 3/4 in. Use pieces of masking tape to mark this overlap.

4. Remove the laminate pieces from the substrate and apply adhesive to all parts.

5. Reapply the guide piece of laminate, making sure it lines up with the pencil mark you traced onto the substrate in Step 3. Use spacer sticks to prevent it from sticking until you have the laminate aligned. Pull out one stick at a time, starting with the edge closest to the pencil line. Use a laminate roller to make sure the laminate is thoroughly pressed down.

6. Apply the overlap piece using the same method. Line it up with the tape on the guide piece, remove the spacer sticks, and roll it down. Roll as close to the seam as you can. This helps prevent chips from getting under the laminate when you rout the seam.

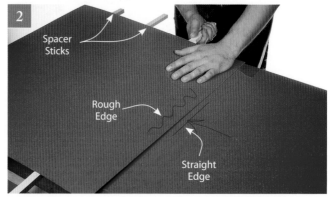

The first step to making a perfect plastic-laminate butt joint is to rout a straight edge on one piece of laminate. Use a straight board as a guide and a flush-trim bit to make the cut.

Apply both pieces of laminate to the substrate. The piece with the straight edge goes down first; the second piece overlaps it by a small amount. Spacer sticks prevent the laminate from sticking to the substrate, making it easy to align the parts.

Rout the joint. Keep the underscribe attachment's lip in constant contact with the bottom piece's straight edge while routing and keep the attachment firmly against the laminate surface.

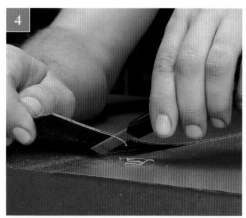

Shave the burr off the bottom edge of the overlap piece with a utility knife.

Press the overlap piece into place using a block of wood. The piece should fit snugly and snap into place.

Also, a vacuum attachment is available for the underscribe attachment. It removes almost all the debris as you rout the seam so is well worth the money.

7. Clean the laminate surface and your router base, because a small piece of debris between the router base and the laminate could cause a nasty scratch. A little paraffin wax on the router base helps it to slide easily.

You're now ready to rout the joint (Photo 3). With the router turned off, position the lip of the underscribe attachment firmly against the straight edge on the guide piece (Fig. A). Turn the router on only after you're sure it's positioned properly. Maintain contact between the lip and the guide piece throughout the cut.

8. Use a utility knife to remove the burr from the bottom edge of the newly trimmed piece (Photo 4). Flick the waste away from the bottom of the joint as you go. Also peek under this piece for any stray chips and remove them. It's paramount that you leave no chips under this piece of laminate or it will not push down level with the first piece.

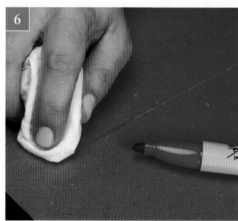

Hide any trace of the seam by applying permanent marker or an oil stain of similar color to the laminate. Wipe off the excess with solvent and a rag.

9. Snap the trimmed piece into place using a wood block with a rounded edge (Photo 5). Use a laminate roller to press the seam down thoroughly.

10. Hide the seam with permanent marker or an oil stain in a color similar to the laminate (Photo 6). Wipe the seam with a solvent, such as denatured alcohol or lacquer thinner, to remove any excess marker or stain on the surface of the laminate.

by BRAD HOLDEN

Tips for Applying Tee Molding

LOOKING FOR A QUICK, EASY WAY TO PUT A DURABLE EDGE ON A PROJECT?

Tee molding might be the perfect answer. Installation could not be simpler: just rout the slot and tap the molding in place. There's no gluing, no ironing, no finishing, and it'll stand up to years of abuse. Used extensively on store and restaurant fixtures, tee molding is also a great choice for shop cabinets, kid's furniture or any other place where a durable, impact-resistant edge is a plus.

Tee molding is available in a huge array of colors and profiles, so let your imagination run wild. Use it to add bright colors to a child's playroom or bedroom. It can transform the ordinary, like a set of laundry room shelves, into a colorful highlight. Check out these eight great installation tips. They'll ensure hassle-free success the first time you try tee molding.

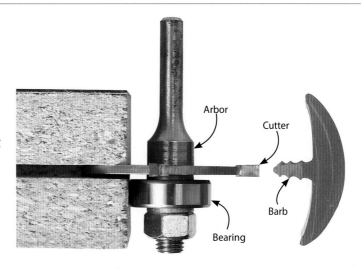

Use the Right Bit

Use the appropriate sized slot cutter to cut the slot for the barb. If the slot is too wide, the barb won't hold properly. If it's too narrow, it can split the substrate. Suppliers specify what size cutter you need for each tee molding—don't cheat. Some manufacturers allow you to swap out different-sized cutters on a single arbor (see photo above). Others sell each cutter size as an individual bit.

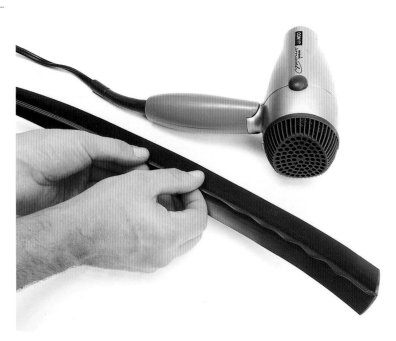

Massage Out the Kinks

Remove kinks in the barb before installation. Tee molding comes in rolled coils that can cause kinks in the barbs. The kinks can get hung up on the substrate slot and make barb insertion a real chore. Use a hair dryer to warm the kinked area. Then massage the kink out. If heat doesn't do the trick, as a last resort you can cut out a kink with a utility knife.

Tap Lightly

Tap tee molding into the slot using a rubber mallet. Use only enough force to seat the molding. You're not pounding in a nail here. Excessive force can cause the molding to compress and stretch. Eventually, it will spring back to its original shape. This could leave gaps along the edges where it was trimmed flush to the surface and at the joints where the ends meet.

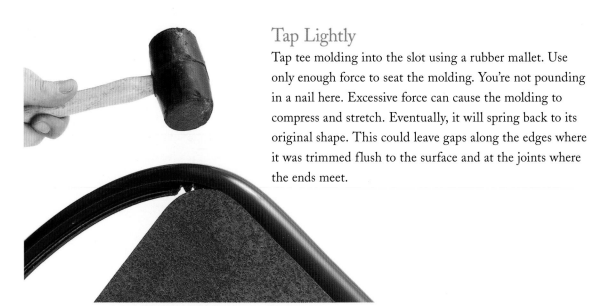

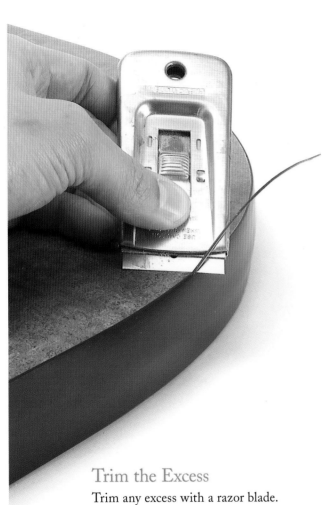

Trim the Excess

Trim any excess with a razor blade.
A straight edge razor in a holder,
as shown, provides the best control.

Notch Around a Tight Curve

Cut "V" shaped notches
in the barb where the tee
molding bends around a corner.
Three or four notches cut with
a utility knife are usually enough.
If you don't notch the corners, the
barb will "bunch up" in the slot
so the molding won't seat properly,
and it could split the substrate.

Warm Up a Tight Bend

Use a hair dryer to install large profile (thick) tee molding around tight corners. A little added warmth makes tee molding much more pliable. Consider room temperature to be a minimum for tee molding installation. Cold molding just won't cooperate when you install it.

Hair Dryer

Make Perfect Butt Joints

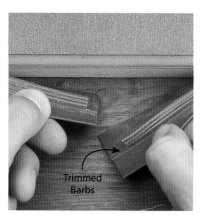

Trimmed Barbs

Cut molding about 1/2 inch longer than needed. Then trim about 1/4 inch off the barbs at each end. Install one end and overlap the other.

Cut through both layers with a utility knife and a straight edge. Keep the knife at 90 degrees to ensure a square cut and a tight joint.

Voila! A perfect joint.

by BRUCE KIEFFER

Wood Edging on Laminated Tops

5 STEPS TO ALIGN AND FINISH WOOD EDGING ON A PLASTIC-LAMINATED SURFACE

Most woodworkers cringe at the thought of applying wood edging to a plastic-laminated top. Unlike wood veneer surfaces, you can't sand this edging flush without scratching the laminate. Over the years, I've discovered a few tricks of the trade that will help you avoid messy glue-ups and misaligned edging.

Even after you've successfully applied the trim, you still face a woodworking conundrum: applying finish to the wood edge but not the laminate. I found a special automotive masking tape that works better than I could imagine. Applying any type of finish is now fast and clean. Just follow these easy steps for a clean-looking, hassle-free top.

Cutting the Miters

The first hurdle is to cut your edging pieces' mitered corners to fit exactly—you can't get away with being a hair short or long. Start with the two long trim pieces. Use a short piece of edging with a mitered end to test-fit the long pieces. Leave the end pieces about 1/16 in. long; they'll be trimmed to fit later. Finish-sand the top edges of the edging pieces before you glue them on. You don't want to sand the top of the trim after it's applied and risk scratching the laminate. After the long runs are glued in place, you can cut and fit the end pieces for airtight miters.

EDITOR: DAVE MUNKITTRICK • ART DIRECTION: VERN JOHNSON • PHOTOGRAPHY: MIKE MAVII

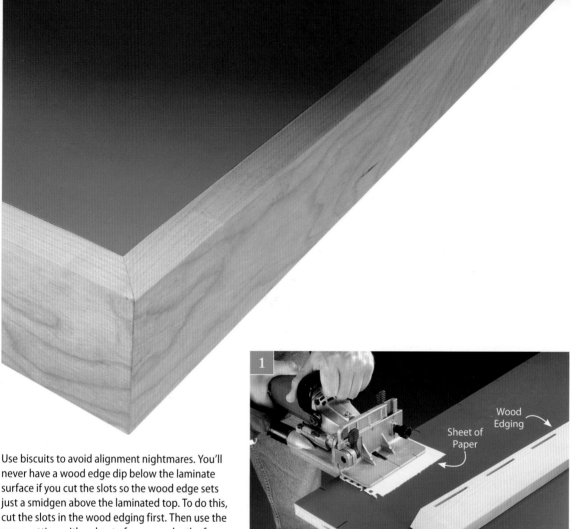

Use biscuits to avoid alignment nightmares. You'll never have a wood edge dip below the laminate surface if you cut the slots so the wood edge sets just a smidgen above the laminated top. To do this, cut the slots in the wood edging first. Then use the same setting with a sheet of paper under the fence to cut the slots in the laminated top. Use No. 20 biscuits and set the slots 4 in. to 6 in. apart.

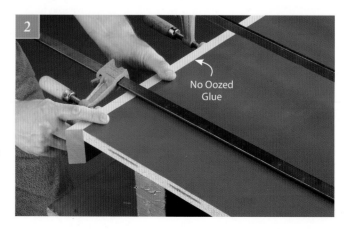

Glue on one piece of edging at a time. Glue-up disasters often result from attempts to glue everything at once. Start with the long edging pieces. After they're set, trim the mitered end pieces for an exact fit (see Photo 3). To eliminate squeeze-out on the laminate surface, apply glue only to the inside of the biscuit slots and a bead along the edge below the biscuits.

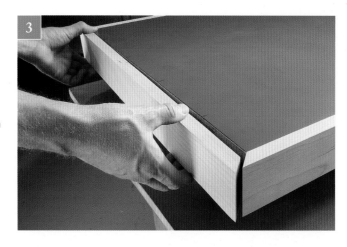

The end pieces are cut slightly oversize and then trimmed to create a tight joint. To trim off a whisker, try this: With the miter saw off, drop the blade down and push the mitered end of the edging up against the teeth with enough pressure to ever so slightly deflect the blade. With a tight hold on the edging, raise the blade back up. Turn the saw on and slowly make the cut. This will take the lightest shaving off the end and allow you to work your way to the perfect fit.

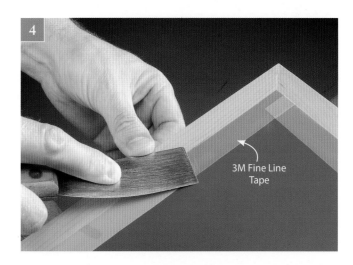

3M Fine Line Tape

Get a clean crisp finish line using 3M's Scotch Fine Line Tape. This is truly a "magic" masking tape! Originally designed for auto bodywork, it makes an airtight seal that no finish can sneak under. Apply the tape to the laminate with your fingers first. Then, to make a tight seal, use a putty knife to slowly, gently press down the tape.

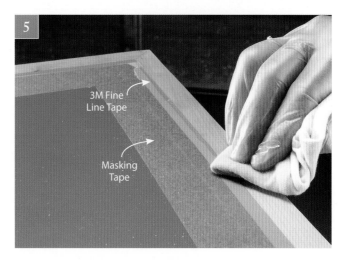

3M Fine Line Tape

Masking Tape

Wipe on two or three coats of Danish oil or brush on varnish or lacquer, you name it—this tape will keep a perfect seal. Overlap a row of 2-in. blue masking tape on the Fine Line tape for an extra layer of protection, or if you're finishing with lacquer, make the overlap using green masking tape formulated for lacquer. Remove the tape after the finish dries. You'll find a sharp finish line and perfectly clean laminate.

Installing Cabinets

E ven though installation is the last major step in completing your cabinet project, it should be one of the first things you think about. This chapter reveals tips for ensuring smooth cabinet installation. For example, even before you cut your first board, make sure your measurements are accurate and verified. Measuring methods vary between cabinetmakers. Some woodworkers prefer a story stick approach, while others simply use a tape measure and record measurements on a sheet of paper. I prefer to use both. When I'm back at my shop, I compare measurements while drawing my plans. Even though discrepancies may mean another trip to the job site, it's better then rebuilding a cabinet. Secondly, before you begin building, always assume the room you're installing cabinets in is out of level and out of plumb. Plan for it by adding a scribe allowance to the sides of your cabinets and counter tops. A third bit of advice is to give your cabinets some breathing room. We woodworkers pride ourselves on cutting joints that fit like pistons, but that will get you into trouble when it comes to fitting cabinets up to, or between, typical house walls.

by TIM JOHNSON

Install Cabinetry and Shelving Like a Pro

TIPS FOR LEVELING, SCRIBING, AND DEALING WITH COMMON OBSTACLES

Does the thought of installing a built-in cabinet make you queasy? You're not alone. Many woodworkers skilled at building free-standing pieces balk when it comes to built-ins. In the workshop, keeping things square assures a good fit and a satisfying result. But in the world of built-ins, square things may have to fit into round holes.

Level, Then Scribe

In the old days, cabinets were literally built in place. Today, built-ins are usually brought to the site partly or completely assembled. They're designed with extra material, called "scribe," added wherever there is a visible joint between the cabinet and the wall, floor or ceiling. This means the stiles, cabinet sides and toe kicks are made extra wide and tops oversized so they can be trimmed. When necessary, one or all of these parts are left off the cabinet until it is installed.

Knowing where to add scribe material and deciding which pieces to leave loose are two critical design elements that are determined in the planning stage. Learning two techniques, how to level a cabinet and how to scribe pieces to fit, will prepare you for most installations.

First map out the location, checking for plumb, level, and square. Make a sketch with exact measurements. On it, indicate corners that are out of square and walls that aren't plumb. Then design the project to fit inside this space, bearing in mind that the cabinet box(es) will be installed first, leveled, scribed, and anchored. Pieces purposefully left off, like the top, are then scribed to fit and added, resulting in a neat, built-in appearance.

First Get Things Level

Map out uneven floors. In any house, old or new, it's risky to assume the floors are level and flat. When installing cabinetry or shelving, it's important to know both how the floor slopes and where the high spots are. Just imagine trying to install floor-to-ceiling bookcases built using a measurement that was taken from a low spot in the floor!

Here's what to do: use level and straight 2x4s to find the highest spot on the area of floor that will be underneath your built-in. Level one 2x4 at the cabinet's back and a second one parallel to it at the cabinet's front. Find the highest point by leveling across these 2x4s front to back. Transfer this point to the wall and use it as a reference for further measurements.

Figure A: Installing Cabinets On A Sloping Floor

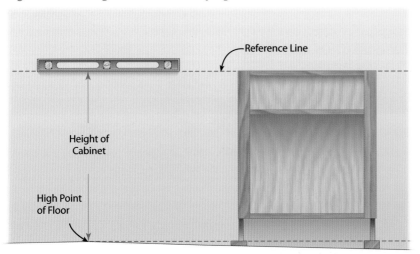

Reference Line

Height of Cabinet

High Point of Floor

Level a row of modular cabinets using a reference line. On a sloping or uneven floor, trying to keep modular cabinets aligned as you level is frustrating and difficult without one. Mark the height of the cabinet on the wall, measuring up from the high point of the floor. Then draw a level line extending the length of the cabinet run.

Align each cabinet back with the reference line you've made on the wall, and use shims to bring it level side-to-side and front-to-back. Shims (right) are your best friends when installing built-ins. They quickly stabilize a cabinet and their narrow wedge shape allows for minute adjustments when leveling.

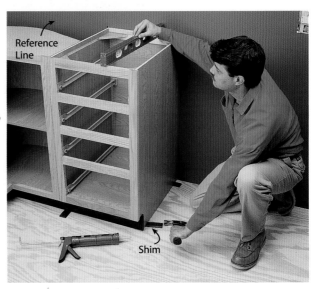

Reference Line

Shim

Separate 2x4 Base

Tarp

Instead of leveling many individual modular cabinets, another option is to make a separate base that spans the entire run. That way you only have to level one unit. Fasten it to the floor after leveling side-to-side and front-to back, then attach cabinet boxes on top. It doesn't matter what you use to make the base—after leveling, everything gets hidden behind a toe-kick made from 1/4-in. plywood. You can scribe this piece to the floor or use a quarter-round molding to cover any gaps.

Then Scribe To Fit

Potential trouble lurks at any visible joint between a cabinet and a wall. Walls are rarely plumb or flat, so gaps between them and the cabinet are likely. Eliminate these gaps by transferring the contours of the wall onto the cabinet so you can cut it to fit. This is called scribing. For a precise fit, it's important the cabinet is exactly positioned and leveled before you scribe it. After scribing, cut, plane, or sand to the line.

When the gaps are small, it's easy to transfer the wall's contour with a carpenter's pencil. Its rectangular shape allows you to make a narrow scribe or a wide scribe, depending on which edge you hold against the wall.

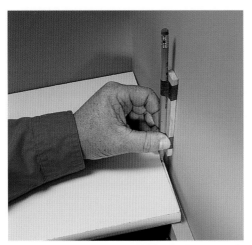

For wider gaps, use a spacer block taped to a pencil. Make the block slightly wider than the largest gap and hold it against the wall as you scribe.

A compass is a versatile scribing tool because it can be adjusted for any size gap, although it's trickier to use than a pencil. It's important to hold a compass locked at the same angle as you scribe. Any variance can result in a poor fit.

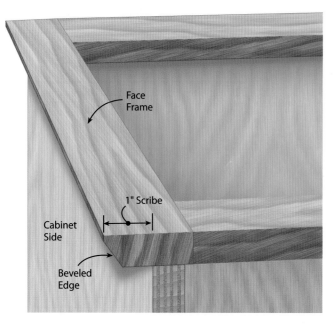

Face Frame

1" Scribe

Cabinet Side

Beveled Edge

When building a cabinet you'll have to add extra material, called "scribe" or "scribing allowance" anywhere the cabinet will meet a wall. On face-frame stiles the scribe is the part that extends beyond the cabinet side.

Most of this material gets cut away when the cabinet is fitted. Scribes usually have a beveled or rabbeted edge so there's less material to remove. Generally, designing one inch scribes into a project is a good idea. It gives you adequate flexibility when fitting and you can always cut it off, which is much easier than adding on!

Figure B: Fitting a Cabinet Between Two Walls

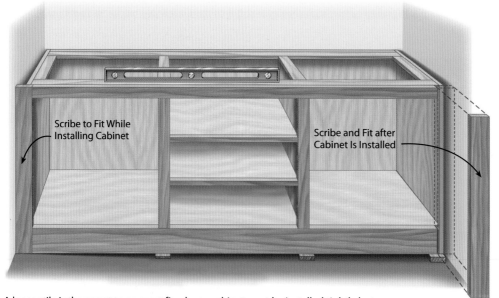

Scribe to Fit While Installing Cabinet

Scribe and Fit after Cabinet Is Installed

A loose stile is the secret to an exact fit when a cabinet must be installed tightly between two walls. Leave one of the outer stiles unattached and fit it last, after the cabinets have been positioned, leveled, scribed, and anchored in place.

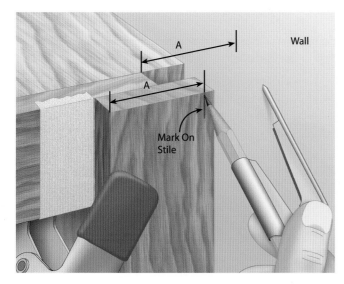

A A Wall

Mark On Stile

How to scribe a loose stile: Measure the greatest distance (a) between the rail and the wall. It could be anywhere along the side of the cabinet. Mark the same distance on the loose stile, measuring from its inner edge. Clamp the stile onto the cabinet, using tape on both rails to position it squarely. Set the compass to span the distance between the wall and the mark on the stile, and scribe the line.

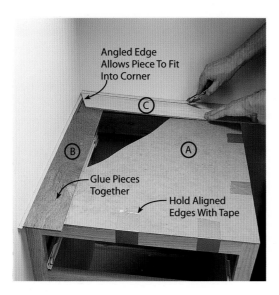

Angled Edge Allows Piece To Fit Into Corner

C

B A

Glue Pieces Together

Hold Aligned Edges With Tape

Scribing two adjacent edges to fit an inside corner is hard. If you scribe one first and then the second, the first no longer fits. Here's a way to fit both edges at once, as shown on this cabinet top: make a pattern from three overlapping pieces, using scraps of thin sheet stock. Align the first piece (a) with the outer edges of the cabinet. Scribe and fit the second piece (b) to one wall and the third piece (c) to the other. Position them precisely and fasten them together with hot-melt glue. Move this pattern onto the top, aligning the outer edges of piece (a) with lines drawn to indicate where the top overhangs the cabinet. Transfer the scribed edges of the pattern onto the top and cut to the lines.

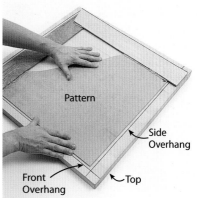

Pattern

Side Overhang

Front Overhang

Top

Use Moldings

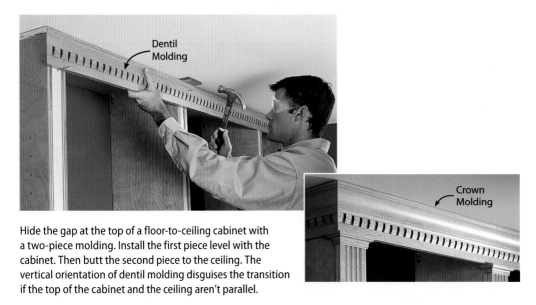

Hide the gap at the top of a floor-to-ceiling cabinet with a two-piece molding. Install the first piece level with the cabinet. Then butt the second piece to the ceiling. The vertical orientation of dentil molding disguises the transition if the top of the cabinet and the ceiling aren't parallel.

Sometimes scribing is tough. Fitting a piece around two outside corners that pinch inward, as this one does, is almost impossible. It's easier to roughly scribe to fit, then cover the gaps with a decorative molding.

Safely Dealing with Outlets and Vents

Most walls have electrical outlets or heating ducts in them. It's easy to safely extend a floor vent (right). Just wear gloves so you don't cut yourself. But electrical outlets must be treated with extreme caution. Always shut off the power at the fuse box or breaker panel before beginning work.

If an outlet is unnecessary and you plan to build over it, it has to be safely disabled first. You can't just remove the receptacle and bury the spliced wires in the wall. To keep an outlet functional and give it a neat, built-in appearance, you'll need to cut a hole in the back of the cabinet, mount the receptacle to its face and install a metal box extender. The extender protects the exposed area, up to a 1-1/4-in. gap, between the wall-mounted electrical box and the receptacle. If you are unfamiliar with electrical work, hire a licensed electrician.

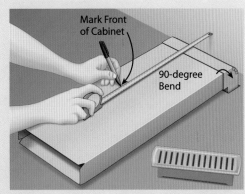

Extend a forced-air duct to the front of the cabinet with a 90-degree bend and a short length of prefabricated duct, cut to length with snips.

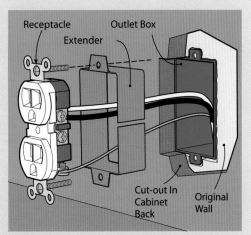

Use a metal box extender to protect combustible material, like wood or plywood when there's a gap between the receptacle and the box. Code requires it. The extender houses the receptacle and extends back inside the electrical box, protecting the exposed cut-out area of the cabinet. After it's wired, two wraps of electrical tape (not shown) around the receptacle will insulate the terminal screws from the metal wall of the extender.

by BRAD HOLDEN

Precision 3-Wall Scribes

A SIMPLE TEMPLATE GUARANTEES A PERFECT FIT

Fitting a countertop between two side walls and a back wall is one of the most challenging installations you will ever face. Experienced cabinetmakers can do this with ease by marking and scribing straight to the countertop, but they have years of experience. I take a more roundabout approach, but it's virtually goof-proof.

I prefer to make a template of the opening and rout my top to match. This prevents trimming too much from any side, which would create a gap that can't easily be repaired. I'll show you a simple method for making this template using a kitchen desktop that butts against a cabinet, a side wall and a back wall as an example. I installed this desktop with no backsplash. If you intend to install a backsplash, you don't need a precise scribe on the back edge.

Materials

You'll need a piece of plywood or MDF slightly smaller than the countertop opening—about 1/4 in. less at each side and the back is sufficient. This board

will be your template's base and will rest on top of the base cabinets or wall cleats. You'll also need three guide boards of any 1/4-in.-thick material. Cut them about 4 in. wide. Make two a couple inches longer than the countertop's depth and one a few inches shorter than the countertop's width.

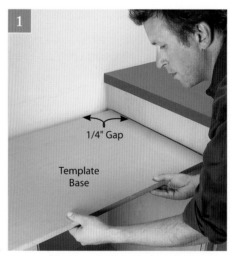

Three-wall scribes are tricky because both ends and the back of the countertop all have to fit snugly. My technique removes most of the difficulty by starting with a loose-fitting template base. I'll scribe three guide boards, one for each wall, and screw them to the template base.

Make the Template

Lay the template base on top of the cabinets or cleats and temporarily secure it with a couple of screws (Photo 1). Position one guide board on either the left or right end and push it up against the side and back wall (Photo 2). Next, you'll need a washer whose rim is big enough to span the widest gap between the wall and the guide board. Put your pencil tip in the washer's hole and draw a line on the guide board, letting the washer follow the wall's contour (Photo 3). Clamp the guide board to

Guide Board

Position the first guide board on the template base by sliding it up against both the side and back wall. It must be long enough to overhang the front of the template base by a couple of inches.

your workbench, and use a belt sander to sand down to the line (Photo 4). Check the fit against the wall. When you've got a snug fit, screw the guide board to the template (Photo 5). Repeat the same steps on the guide boards on the other side and on the back. Cut the back guide board so it fits between the two side guide boards. Make a mark on the side guide boards to indicate where you want the front edge of the countertop to line up (Photo 6). Then, remove the template assembly and set it on the countertop to be trimmed. Line up the marks you made with the front edge of the countertop, and clamp the template in place (Photo 7). Note: Build your countertop about 3/8 in. larger in width and depth than the opening.

Rout the Top

Using a top-bearing pattern bit with a cutting length at least 1-1/2 in. long, trim around the template (Photo 8). Stop short of the front left corner so you don't blow it out, and carefully finish the cut with a belt sander (Photo 9).

Tilt the countertop into place (Photo 10). It should fit snugly, but if it's too tight, you may need to adjust the fit slightly. To do this, reattach the template slightly off center and rout the exposed edge to gain a little clearance. If you follow these steps carefully, you'll end up with a perfect fit.

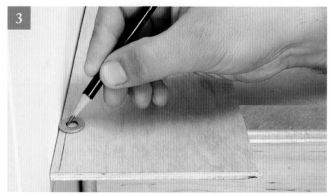

Along the side and back wall, mark a scribe line on the guide board using a pencil and a small washer. The washer follows any bumps or curves in the wall. Repeat this step with a second guide board on the other side.

Clamp the guide board on your workbench and carefully sand to the pencil line. When you're done, check the fit against the wall. The beauty of this method is that if the fit's not quite right, you can just mark and sand again.

Screw the scribed side guide boards to the template base. Mark, sand, and attach the back guide board last, because it butts between the two side guide boards.

Mark both side guide boards at the exact point where you want the front edge of the countertop located. This mark will be used to accurately align the guide boards on the countertop.

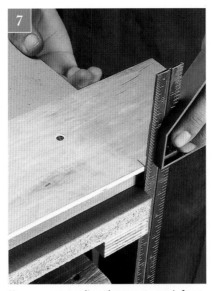

Use a square to align the countertop's front edge with the marks on the side guide boards. The countertop must be slightly larger than the template assembly.

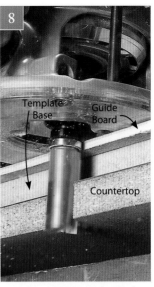

Rout the countertop's finished shape using a top-bearing pattern bit. Start at the countertop's front right corner and rout counterclockwise.

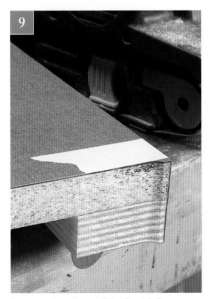

Stop routing short of the front left corner and use a belt sander to remove the remaining material. This prevents the router bit from chipping out the front edge. A piece of masking tape provides a clear mark where to stop sanding.

Tilt the counter into place. Fasten it with screws from underneath through the top of the base cabinet. A wood cleat screwed to the right-hand cabinet supports this top on the right side.

WORKSHOP TIPS

Temporary Support
Board

Solo Cabinet Hanging

Hanging a wall cabinet is usually a two-person job—one to hold the cabinet level
and one to screw it to the wall. I'm nearly always working alone, so I came up with
this safe way to wall-mount a cabinet by myself.

Screw a 2x4 to the wall to rest the cabinet on and screw the cabinet to the wall.
As long as the 2x4 is level and at the right height, all should go well. When you
remove the 2x4 you will have a couple of holes to repair but it's a small price to pay
for the hassle you'll avoid.

M. Sue Smelser

Fitting a Frameless Cabinet into a Corner

Q I plan to build and install frameless European-style cabinets in my kitchen. I know how to scribe face-frame cabinets to fit into corners but, from what I've seen, there's nothing to scribe on a frameless cabinet. How's it done?

A It's actually pretty easy. What you do is attach a scribe to the end of the cabinet that goes into the corner. The scribe does several things: It moves the end of the cabinet away from the wall so the door can open past 90 degrees. It also provides a thin edge that's easy to trim for a tight fit against the wall. Finally, it gives a cabinet run a nice finished look where it meets a wall.

Typically, the scribe face is made 1 to 1-1/2 in. wide, but you're free to do what you think looks best. Cut a rabbet on the edge of the face piece that fits against the wall. Trim the rabbeted edge until it fits snugly and plumb on the wall where the cabinet will hang. Glue a screw flange onto the back of the face piece, screw the scribe to the cabinet and hang.

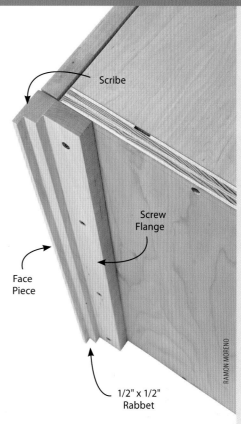

Scribe

Screw Flange

Face Piece

1/2" x 1/2" Rabbet

RAMON MORENO

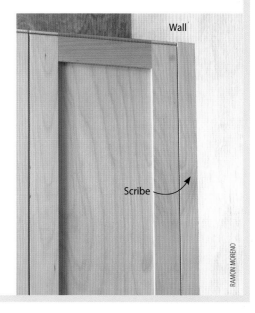

Wall

Scribe

RAMON MORENO

QUESTION & ANSWER

How Can I Retrofit Vertical Dividers in a Kitchen Cabinet?

Q My wife is an avid baker. I'd love to surprise her by adding some vertical dividers in a base cabinet for storing all her cookie sheets and cake pans. Is there a simple way to do it without taking anything apart?

Roger Espinoza

A Sure! Here's how to earn some quick brownie points: Mount a set of wire-shelf supports at the top and bottom of the cabinet interior. It just takes a couple of 1/8-in. holes for each support. You may have to add a board to build down the top of the cabinet opening so it's flush with the door opening of the cabinet. Then run 1/8-in. dadoes along the ends of each divider, glue hardwood edging to the front edge and slide them home. It's that easy! Now she'll have perfect storage for all those cookie sheets, cake pans, and trays.

Added Boards

Divider

Wire-Shelf Support

1/8" Dado

RAMON MORENO

Universal Slide Jig

I've tried all kinds of jigs for installing drawer slides, none to my satisfaction. But my new jig holds the drawer slides right where I want while I install them.

You can make this jig for any size cabinet. For standard base cabinets, cut four strips of 3/4" plywood, 3" wide. Cut two of the strips 30" long for the base and the crossbar; cut the other two 38" long for the legs.

Next rout 3/8" x 34" long slots into the legs, so the jig is infinitely adjustable. Then, glue and screw the legs to the base, offsetting them 1/4" from the base's edge so the crossbar sits flat against the cabinet side even when you have a slide mounted on the cabinet's bottom.

The crossbar spans the two legs and is held in place with 1/4" by 2" bolts and 1/4–20 jig knobs. Counterbore the bolts so they don't scratch the cabinet sides. The jig extends past the front of the cabinet so you can get at the front slide screws.

To use the jig, mark your drawer heights at the front and back of the cabinet. Stand the jig in the cabinet and position the crossbar to hold the first slide. Then just flip the jig around to the other side to install the first slide's mate.

Rod Wolfington

EDITOR: BRAD HOLDEN • PHOTOGRAPHS COURTESY OF CONTRIBUTOR UNLESS NOTED

Cabinetmaking Projects

M aybe you don't need a new kitchen; maybe you just need some more storage space. This section contains 10 kitchen upgrades that add storage and convenience to your existing kitchen. You'll find ways to store your many pots, pans, utensils, small appliances, cleaning supplies, and food. There's a mini pantry for your canned goods, a pull-out trash or recycling drawer, add-on shelves for cleaning supplies, and a very handy appliance garage. (Who doesn't need another garage?) If you travel with your cakes and casseroles, the portable food safe will easily protect them along the way and help you to deliver them in style. For a simple, fun kitchen project that also makes a handy gift, check out the wooden salad tongs. If you want to learn some tricks about designing a built-in cabinet, then take a closer look at the handsome sycamore cabinet. Or if you need some additional seating for your kitchen, the kitchen stool project is a great choice. The kitchen stool is designed so you don't need a lathe to make the legs, just some creative router work. A router is also used to give the seat's comfortable shape.

by MAC WENTZ

Simple Kitchen Upgrades

THREE EASY PROJECTS THAT ADD STORAGE AND CONVENIENCE

Drawers and Slides for Old Cabinets

If your old drawers are coming apart, here's a way to build new boxes and save the drawer faces: Rabbeted corners and a bottom that slips into dadoes make for quick, simple, sturdy construction (Fig. A).

You can reuse the old slides, or you can upgrade to ball-bearing slides. Ball-bearing slides allow full extension and provide years of smooth, quiet service. These slides are more expensive, $15

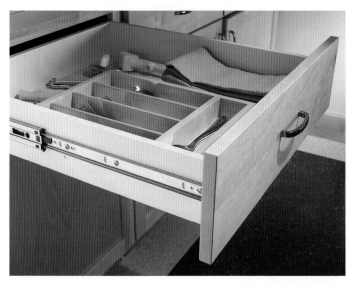

or more per set of 22-inch slides, but worth it, especially for large or heavily loaded drawers.

If you upgrade the slides, your new box may need to be slightly different in width from the old. To determine the drawer width, carefully measure the width of the cabinet opening and subtract 1 in. to allow for the slides. The slides shown here require at least 1 in. of clearance (1/2 in. per side) and no more than 1-1/16 in. Since correcting a drawer that's too narrow is a lot easier than correcting one that's too wide, I allow 1-1/16 in. of clearance (see Oops! page 206). If your cabinets have face frames, you'll need mounting blocks inside the cabinet to provide surfaces that are flush with the inside of the face frame (Photos 2 and 3).

Begin by ripping plywood into strips for the drawer box front, back, and sides, but don't cut them to length just yet. Cut dadoes in the plywood strips by making overlapping passes with your tablesaw blade. You're not going for a squeaky-tight fit here; the 1/4-in.

EDITOR: DAVE MUNKITTRICK • ART DIRECTION: PATRICK HUNTER • PHOTOGRAPHY: BILL ZUEHLKE • ILLUSTRATION: FRANK ROHRBACH

plywood bottoms should slip easily into the dado.

Cut the strips to length for the drawer sides and rabbet the ends. Use the completed sides to determine the length of the front and back pieces. Cut the drawer bottoms from 1/4-in. plywood, undersizing them by about 1/16 in.

Assemble the drawer using glue at the corner joints (Photo 1). The bottom is held by dadoes, so there's no need to glue it.

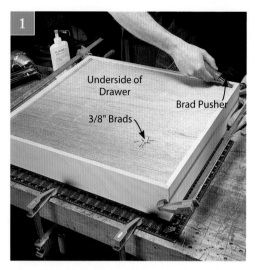

Assemble and square the drawer box. For no-fuss squaring, try this: With clamps in place, nudge the drawer against a framing square and push a brad through the bottom near each corner. Unless your brad nailer shoots 3/8-in. brads, a brad pusher is the best tool for this.

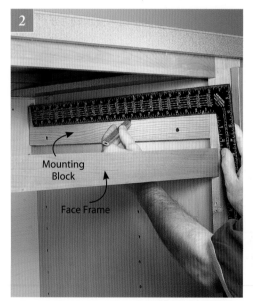

Mark a "screw line" on a mounting block screwed to the inside of the cabinet. You'll position the slide by driving screws through the line. The location of the line isn't critical—the slides will work fine whether they're mounted high, low or in the middle of the drawer side. But the line must be square to the cabinet front.

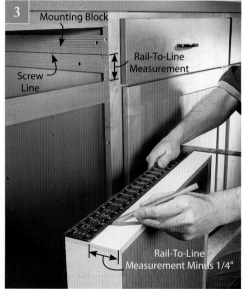

Mark screw lines on the drawer sides. First, measure from the face frame rail to the screw line on the mounting block. Then subtract 1/4 in. and measure from the bottom edge of the drawer box to determine the placement of the screw lines on the drawer. That way, the drawer will have 1/4-in. clearance above the rail.

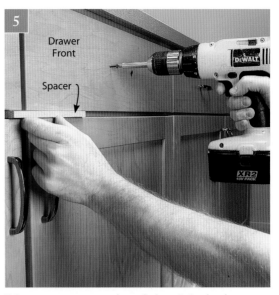

Fasten the slides by driving screws into the screw lines. The slides pull apart for easy mounting. Begin by using only the vertical slots on the drawer member and the horizontal slots on the cabinet member. This lets you adjust the drawer's fit before adding more screws.

Drive temporary screws through the existing hardware holes into the drawer box. Then pull out the drawer and attach the front with permanent screws from inside. A spacer positions the drawer front evenly.

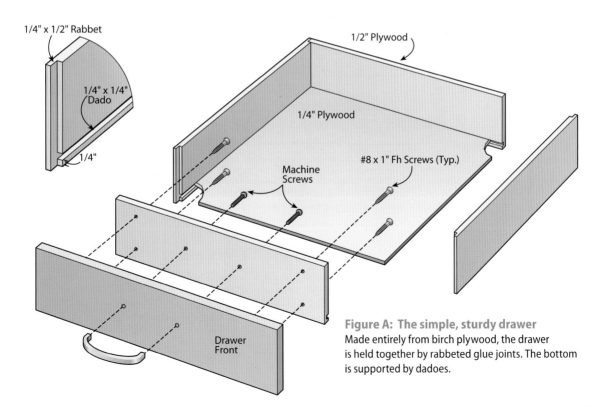

Figure A: The simple, sturdy drawer
Made entirely from birch plywood, the drawer is held together by rabbeted glue joints. The bottom is supported by dadoes.

Toe-Kick Drawers

I always looked at the toe space under the cabinets in my too-small kitchen and thought it would be a great place to add drawers. After some head scratching, I found a way to do it without having to install drawer slides in that dark, cramped space. I mounted the drawer and slides in a self-contained cradle that slips easily under the cabinet (Fig. B). Because the cabinet overhangs the toe-kick by 3 or 4 in., full-extension slides are a necessity for this project. Better yet, use "overtravel" slides that extend an extra inch.

The toe-kick under the cabinets shown here was just a strip of 1/4-in. plywood backed by 5/8-in. particleboard (Photo 1). You might run into something different, like particleboard without any backing at all. In any case, opening up the space under the cabinet is usually fairly easy.

Backing

Drywall Saw

Pry off the toe-kick and remove the backing by drilling a large hole near the center, cutting the backing in half and tearing it out. Then grab a flashlight and check for blocks, protruding screws, or anything else that might interfere with the drawer.

To determine the dimensions of the cradle, measure the depth and width of the space and subtract 1/16 in. from both to provide some adjustment room. If your floor covering is thicker than 1/4 in. (ceramic tile, for example) you may have to glue plywood scraps to the underside of the cradle to raise it and prevent the drawer from scraping against the floor when extended. Size the drawer to allow for slides and the cradle's sides.

You'll have to make drawer fronts and attach them to the boxes using the method shown in Photo 5, page 203. Don't worry too much about an exact match of the finish with your existing cabinets. In that dark toe space, nobody will be able to tell. For hardware, consider handles instead of knobs so you can pull the drawers open with your toe.

Build a cradle, simply two sides and a bottom, to hold the drawer. Attach the cradle's sides to the slides and drawer, then add the plywood bottom.

Slip the cradle under the cabinet. Then drive a pair of screws through each side and into the cabinet box as far back as you can reach.

Figure B: Toe-kick drawer and cradle
A drawer mounted in a cradle forms
a self-contained unit that slips under
a base cabinet.

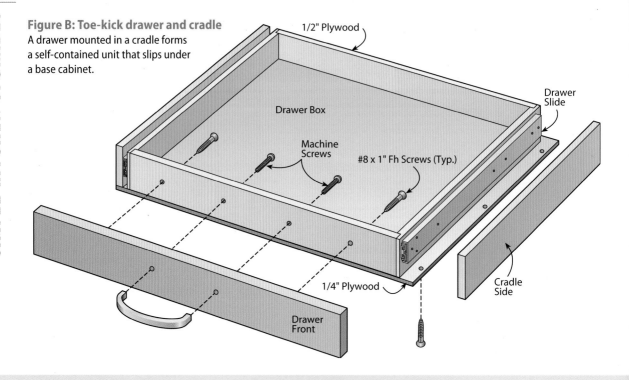

1/2" Plywood

Drawer
Slide

Drawer Box

Machine
Screws

#8 x 1" Fh Screws (Typ.)

1/4" Plywood

Cradle
Side

Drawer
Front

Oops!

The manufacturer of these slides says that the
drawer box must be between 1-in. and
1-1/16-in. narrower than the drawer opening.
They're not kidding. I learned the hard way
that a drawer that falls outside this range won't
slide smoothly no matter how much grease
or brute force you apply.

   With such a small margin for error,
occasional mistakes are inevitable. And I've
found that it's better to err on the too-narrow
side of that margin. If a drawer turns out a tad
too wide, you have to sand down the sides or route a super-shallow
dado to recess the slide. Both are a pain. But if the drawer comes
out a hair too narrow, a few layers of tape applied to the back of
the drawer member is all that's needed. So I'm now in the habit
of making drawers 1-1/16 in. (instead of just 1 in.) narrower than
the opening. Most of the time they glide perfectly. And when they
don't, I just grab the masking tape for a quick, easy fix.

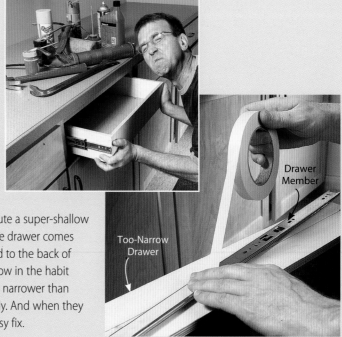

Drawer
Member

Too-Narrow
Drawer

You'll also need iron-on edge banding to cover the exposed edges (Photo 2). When cutting the platform to width, subtract 1/16-in. to allow for the width of the edge banding.

Drawer slides rated for 75- or 100-lb. loads are fine for most drawers. But since this drawer will get more use than most, 120-lb. slides are a good idea.

If the back of your cabinet door is a flat surface, you can run strips of double-faced tape across the front, stick the door in place and fasten it with four small "L" brackets. The back of the door shown here has a recessed panel, so getting it positioned right was a trial-and-error process. Before removing the door, I cut blocks that fit between the door and the floor. Then I

Pull-Out Trash Drawer

Whoever decreed that the trash can goes under the sink got it wrong. With plumbing in the way, there's no space for a good-size can. Plus who likes to bend over and reach into the cabinet?

Here's a great alternative: In one cabinet, replace the shelves with a simple trash can holder mounted on drawer slides. By attaching the existing cabinet door to the front of the pull-out unit, you create a convenient trash drawer. Fig. C and the photos at right show how to build the unit.

Melamine board—particleboard with a tough plastic coating—is a good material for this project because it's easy to clean and inexpensive. The melamine coating, however, tends to chip during cutting. This chipping is worst where the saw teeth exit the material. So with a jigsaw, for example, the face-up side of the sheet will chip. Plan ahead so the chipped edges are out of view.

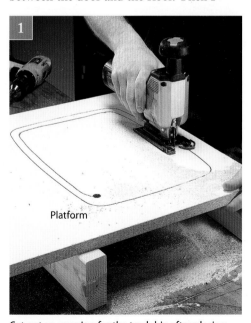

Cut out an opening for the trash bin after placing the bin upside down and tracing around the rim. To allow for the rim, cut about 1/2-in. inside the outline, then check the fit and enlarge the opening as needed.

extended the unit, rested the door on the blocks, and attached two brackets. The resulting fit wasn't quite perfect, so I moved the brackets slightly, checked again and added the remaining brackets.

Edge band the melamine and file away the excess edge banding. To avoid loosening the banding, cut only as you push the file forward, not as you pull back. If you do loosen the edge banding, just reapply with the iron.

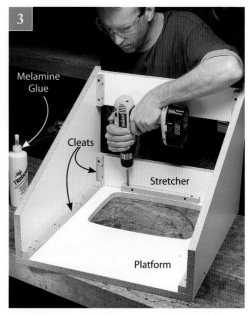

Assemble the unit with screws and 3/4-in. x 3/4-in. cleats. Be sure to use coarse-threaded screws; fine threads won't hold in particleboard. For extra strength, you can use glue that's made especially for melamine's slick surface.

Figure C: Pull-out trash drawer
Made from melamine-coated particleboard, this trash drawer is simple enough to build and install in a day.

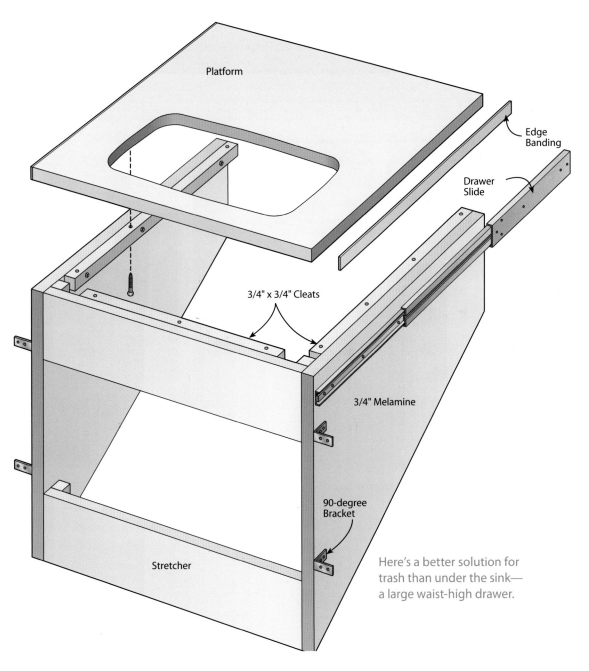

Platform

Edge Banding

Drawer Slide

3/4" x 3/4" Cleats

3/4" Melamine

90-degree Bracket

Stretcher

Here's a better solution for trash than under the sink—a large waist-high drawer.

Weekend Kitchen Projects

HERE ARE THREE WAYS TO IMPROVE STORAGE SPACE IN ANY KITCHEN

Store Knives within Easy Reach!

This countertop knife rack stores a complete set of knives right where you need them. The lipped edges conceal a hole you cut in the countertop. You can easily remove the rack for cleaning.

Keep Cleaning Supplies at Your Fingertips!

Want a sink cabinet shelf that's better than store-bought plastic or wire racks? Make one that mounts securely to the frame of your paneled door, has the same look as your cabinet and maximizes space because it's custom fit.

Reach That Stuff in the Back!

Roll-out kitchen trays replace awkward, deep shelves. They'll fit in any cabinet, are adjustable in height and are especially handy for older or disabled people. Budget at least $60 per cabinet for the hardware and wood.

You can whip through each project in an afternoon, using only a tablesaw and a plunge router.

EDITORS: TOM CASPAR, DAVID RADTKE AND ART ROOTZ • ART DIRECTION: PATRICK HUNTER, MARCIA WILLSTON AND BOB INGAR • PHOTOGRAPHY: BILL ZUEHLKE • ILLUSTRATION: RON CHAMBERLAIN

Countertop Knife Rack

Store up to nine knives in a handy rack that puts sharp edges out of the reach of children. We've arranged the slots to fit a particular set of knives (Fig. A), but you can alter the pattern to suit your set. Experiment by cutting slots in a piece of cardboard. Then make the rack from any hardwood you like. After cutting, sand the rack smooth and finish it with three coats of spray polyurethane. A spray finish is easy to get into the knife slots.

Install a knife-blade shield under the counter (Fig. B and Photo 4). You may need to slightly shorten a drawer to make room for the shield. Also, make sure the shield doesn't interfere with the drawer slides.

Figure A: Knife Rack Layout

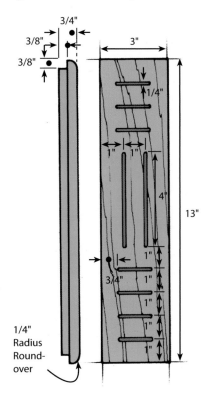

Mark the rack's outline and the knife slot locations on an oversized piece of hardwood. An oversized board provides support for your router and room to clamp a guide board.

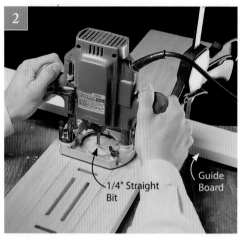

Cut the knife slots with a plunge router. Cut out the rack, round over the top edges with a router and cut rabbets around the bottom edges to form lips.

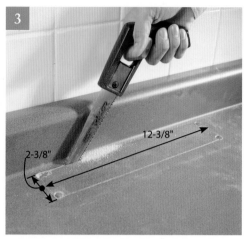

Cut an opening in your countertop with a keyhole saw. Lay out the opening far enough from the backsplash so the lips of the knife rack sit flat on the countertop. Then drill holes in the corners and saw away. (You may have enough room to use a jigsaw to make the long cut farthest from the backsplash.) Add a couple dabs of silicone caulk to the sides of the rack so it fits tight in the slightly oversized opening.

Figure B: Knife Blade Shield

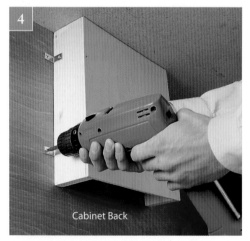

Fasten a blade shield to the back of the cabinet, underneath the knife rack. Build the shield from 1/4-in. plywood and 3/4-in. solid wood.

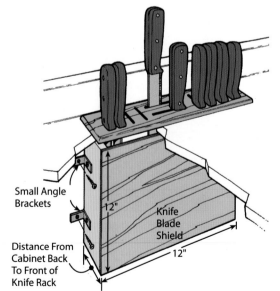

Sink Cabinet Shelf

It's easy to customize this catchall shelf to fit your cabinet doors. Measure the opening of your cabinet (not the door!) and plug your numbers into the Cutting List, page 214. The shelf unit clears the opening by 1/4-in. on all sides.

You can mount this shelf on a cabinet door made of plywood or a door with a raised panel. Solid mounting strips get screwed into the stiles of the door, not the thinner panel.

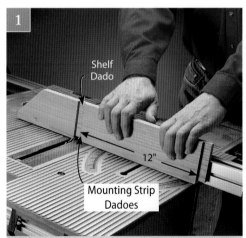

Caution! The blade guard must be removed for this step. **Be careful.**

Cut two pairs of 3/4-in.-wide, 1/4-in.-deep dadoes in the sides; a pair for the two shelves and a pair for the mounting strips. Line up the mounting-strip dado with the shelf dado.

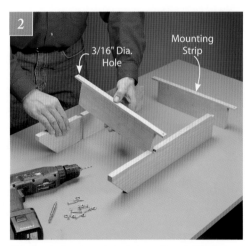

Slip the shelves into their dadoes. First drill holes for the mounting screws 3/8-in. from the end of the mounting strips. Glue the mounting strips to the shelves. Drill pilot holes in the sides and fasten the shelves with long screws.

If you have small children, be sure that cabinets containing cleaning products and other toxic substances have childproof latches attached.

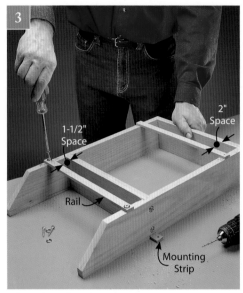

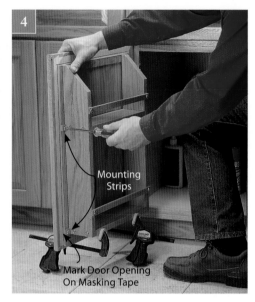

Fasten the rails to the front of the shelves with short screws. Finish washers save you the trouble of perfectly countersinking each hole!

Clamp and screw the shelves to your door, using 3/4-in. screws and finish washers. You may need to add a third hinge and a magnetic catch if the weight of the loaded shelves prevents the door from closing easily.

Hardware

Eight 1-1/4" #8 Oval-Head Wood Screws
Eight 3/4" #8 Oval-Head Wood Screws
16 Finish Washers

Cutting List				
Name	**Qty.**	**Th**	**W**	**L**
Sides	2	3/4"	3-1/2"	1/2" less than height of cabinet opening
Shelves	2	3/4"	3-1/4"	3" less than width of cabinet opening
Rails	2	1/4"	3/4"	1" more than shelves
Mounting Strips	2	1/4"	3/4"	2-1/2" more than shelves

Roll-Out Kitchen Trays

Trays on wheels put all the pots and pans in a deep cabinet within easy reach. If your doors can't open more than 90-degrees, plan on making the horizontal supports wider than shown here. There must be 1/4-in. clearance between the slides and the inside faces of your doors.

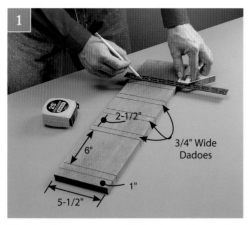

Mark the dadoes on one wide hardwood board. The four upper dadoes make the top shelf adjustable.

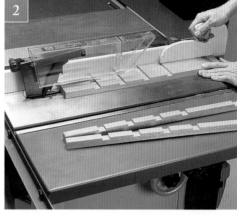

Cut dadoes 1/4-in. deep, then rip the wide board into four vertical supports. Cut horizontal supports to hold the slides.

Glue the vertical supports in place with a couple dabs of construction adhesive. Then fit the horizontal supports tightly in the dadoes, without glue. The horizontal supports must stick out at least 1/4 in. beyond the face frame of your cabinet door. You'll need this clearance for the drawer side to travel freely.

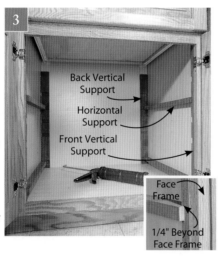

Build the plywood trays with plywood or hardwood sides. The corners may be simply butted together. Align the slide's drawer members flush with the front of the tray.

Fasten the slides to the trays and the horizontal supports. Place the rear end of the cabinet member at least 1/4 in. away from the end of the horizontal support.

Hardware

Two pairs of Euro-style, epoxy-coated drawer slides. They should be 2" shorter than the overall depth of your cabinet. Standard base cabinets are 24" deep. Slides are sold in increments of 2" from 12" to 24."

Cutting List

Name	Qty.	Material	Th	W	L
Front vertical supports	2	Hardwood	3/4"	3/4"	Height of cabinet
Back vertical supports	2	Hardwood	3/4"	1-3/4"	Height of cabinet
Horizontal supports	4	Hardwood	3/4"	1"	About 1" less
Tray bottom	2	Plywood	3/4"	*	**
Tray sides	4	Hardwood	3/4"	2-1/4"	To fit tray

* Width is about 3" less than the cabinet opening. To figure the tray bottom's exact width, subtract the combined thickness of two sides plus 1" from the distance between the installed horizontal supports.

** Length is 2-1/2" less than cabinet depth, measured from the back of the cabinet to the back of the face frame.

by ERIC SMITH *and* DAVID RADTKE

3 More Kitchen Storage Projects

SQUEEZE MORE SPACE FROM YOUR CABINETS WITH CUSTOMIZED ROLL-OUTS

I t may seem like a paradox, but even kitchens that are overflowing have underutilized space. Many base cabinets are only half used, because the back is inaccessible, stuffed with long-forgotten items you can't see unless you get down on your knees with a flashlight. Here's a set of pull-outs that bring everything within reach.

EDITOR: DAVE MUNKITTRICK • ART DIRECTION: EVANGELINE EKBERG AND MARCIA WRIGHT ROEPKE • PHOTOGRAPHY: RAMON MORENO AND BILL ZUEHLKE • ILLUSTRATION: FRANK ROHRBACH

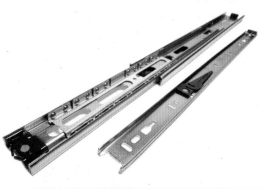

1. Under-Sink Storage

To begin, measure the areas of open space around the plumbing. You may only be able to put a single pull-out on one side, or you may have to shorten them or build them around pipes coming up through the base.

Materials

To make the trays shown here, you'll need a half sheet of 3/4-in. hardwood plywood, 2-ft. x 2-ft. of 1/2-in. plywood, 17 lineal ft. of 1-in. x 4-in. maple, 2 lineal ft. of 1-in. x 6-in. maple, four pairs of 20-in. full-extension ball-bearing slides, a box of 1-5/8-in. screws, wood glue, and construction adhesive.

Bottom Pull-Outs

Measure the frame opening and cut the base (A) 1/4 in. narrower (Fig. A, page 218). Make the drawers 1 in. narrower than the opening between the partitions. Cut and assemble the base assembly (A, B) and drawer parts (C, D, E). Sand and apply two coats of finish to the base and drawers.

Set the drawer slides on 3/4-in. spacers flush with the front edge of the partition (B). Screw them to the partitions; then pull out the drawer members. Set the drawer members on the same 3/4-in. spacers to create the proper bottom clearance for the tray, and screw them to the sides of the trays flush to the fronts. Screw the base assembly to the bottom of the cabinet (Photo 1). Slide in the drawers.

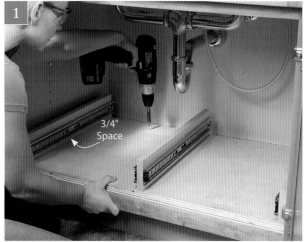

Build and install a base assembly for the bottom pull-outs. Center the base assembly in the cabinet just behind the hinges. Align the front edge with the face frame and screw it to the bottom of the cabinet.

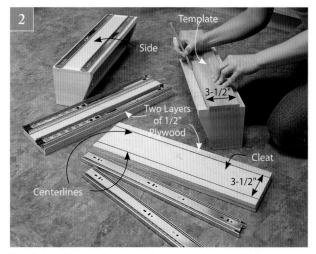

Install the slides on the side pull-out trays. Center a 3-1/2-in. template on the cleat and the tall side of each tray and trace the edges. Center the mounting holes of the slides on these lines.

Side-Mounted Pull-Outs

Make the side support cleats (K) so they sit flush or slightly proud of the face frame. Check for hinges that might get in the way of the pull-out tray. Assemble the trays with glue and screws. Apply finish.

Attach the slides and mount them in the cabinet (Photos 2 and 3). Scuff the cabinet side with sandpaper and use construction adhesive and screws to hold the cleats. Cabinet sides are often finished, so screws alone may not hold well.

3

Temporary Spacer

Attach the support cleats to the side of the cabinet using screws and construction adhesive. Use a temporary plywood spacer to hold each cleat in position.

Cutting List

Part	Name	Qty.	Dimensions (Th x W x L)
A	Plywood base	1	3/4" x 32-3/4" x 20"
B	Base partition	3	3/4" x 3-1/2" x 20"
C	Plywood tray bottom	2	3/4" x 12-3/4" x 18-1/2"
D	Tray side	4	3/4" x 3-1/2" x 18-1/2"
E	Tray front and back	4	3/4" x 3-1/2" x 14-1/4"
F	Upper tray bottom	2	1/2" x 5-1/2" x 18-1/2"
G	Plywood upper tray side	2	3/4" x 5" x 18-1/2"
H	Plywood upper tray side	2	3/4" x 3" x 18-1/2"
J	Upper tray front, back	4	3/4" x 5-1/2" x 5-1/2"
K	Side cleat, double layer	4	1/2" x 5-1/2" x 20"

Figure A: Under-Sink Storage Exploded View

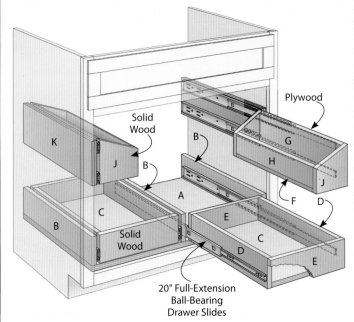

Plywood

Solid Wood

K

J

B

B

G

H

J

A

F

D

C

B

E

C

Solid Wood

D

E

20" Full-Extension Ball-Bearing Drawer Slides

2. Mini-Pantry

These pull-outs bring boxes, jars, and cans within easy reach. To build this mini-pantry, you'll need two sheets of 3/4-in. hardwood plywood (I used Baltic birch for its attractive edge) and two pairs of 20-in. full-extension ball-bearing slides.

Start by building a box to fit inside the cabinet. Measure the frame opening and subtract 1/4 in. to get the box's outside dimensions. I made this pantry for a 24-in. base cabinet, so change the cutting list to fit your base. Also keep in mind that most 3/4-in. plywood actually measures 23/32 in.

Cut the box parts (A, B, C) and assemble them with glue and screws (Fig. B, below). Find the drawers' width by subtracting 1 in. from the openings in the box.

Figure B: Mini-Pantry Exploded View

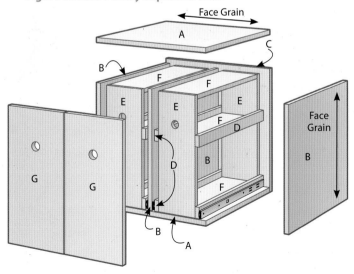

Cutting List

Overall Dimensions: 20-1/4"H x 20-3/4"W x 22"D

Part	Name	Qty.	Dimensions (Th x W x L)
A	Base and top	2	3/4" x 20-1/2" x 20-3/4"
B	Sides and center	3	3/4" x 20-1/2" x 18-13/16"
C	Back	1	3/4" x 20-3/4" x 20-1/4"
D	Shelf side	8	3/4" x 1-3/4" x 20-1/4"
E	Drawer front and back	4	3/4" x 6-7/8" x 18-1/2"
F	Drawer top, bottom, shelf	6	3/4" x 6-7/8" x 18-3/4"
G	Drawer face	2	3/4" x 9-3/4" x 19-3/4"

Cut all the pieces for the drawers (D, E, F, G). Soften the edges of the drawer sides (D) and drawer face (G) using a 1/4-in. round-over bit. Assemble the drawer parts (D, E, F) with screws and glue. Position the center shelf (F) at the height you prefer. Attach the sides (D) with finish nails and glue.

Set the drawer slides on the bottom of the box. Align the slides with the front edge and attach. Remove the drawer member and screw it to the drawer side 1/4 in. above the bottom.

Install the box (see photo, right). Install the drawers. Center the drawer faces (G) on the drawers and screw them from the inside. Drill 1-1/2-in.-dia. holes for finger pulls or attach shallow pulls. Apply two coats of finish.

Build a box for the drawers to fit inside the base cabinet. Remove the cabinet doors and slide the box into the cabinet. Screw the box securely to the bottom of the cabinet.

3. Under-Cabinet Drawer

Unused space often sits in plain view under the upper cabinets. This pull-out is perfect for storing knives or coupons. You'll need 8 lineal ft. of 3/4-in. x 1-3/4-in. hardwood that matches your cabinet, 2 lineal ft. of 1-1/8-in. x 1-1/8-in. hardwood, 1 ft. x 2 ft. of 1/4-in. hardwood plywood and one pair of 12-in. full-extension drawer slides.

Measure the space under the cabinet. Cut the supports (G) to fit this space and protrude about 1/16 in. below the cabinet. Size the drawer by subtracting 2-1/2 in.— 1 in. for the slides and 1-1/2 in. for the two fixed sides (D). The front-to-back dimension is the minimum required for a 12-in. drawer slide.

Cut the drawer parts (A, B, C, E). Assemble the drawer using pocket screws or glue and finish nails. Rout the bottom of the drawer frame with a 3/8-in. rabbeting bit set 1/4 in. deep. Square the corners with a chisel. Then nail in the plywood bottom with 3/4-in. brad nails. Draw a centerline 3/4 in. up from the bottom edge on the fixed sides (D) and the drawer sides (B). Screw on the drawer slides, flush to the front.

Glue and screw the under-cabinet supports to the fixed sides. Install the drawer assembly (see photo, right). Glue the drawer pull (F) in the center behind the drawer front. Then finish the drawer to match the cabinet.

Install the completed drawer assembly. Clamp it to the cabinet and fasten it with screws from above.

Cutting List

Part	Name	Qty.	Dimensions (Th x W x L)
A	Drawer front	1	3/4" x 1-3/4" x 20-1/2"
B	Drawer side	2	3/4" x 1-3/4" x 11-7/8"
C	Drawer back	1	3/4" x 1-3/4" x 15-1/2"
D	Fixed side	2	3/4" x 1-3/4" x 11-7/8"
E	Drawer bottom	1	1/4" x 16-1/8" x 11-3/4"
F	Drawer pull	1	1/2" x 1/2" x 5"
G	Support	2	1-3/16" x 1-1/8" x 10-3/4"

Figure C: Under-Cabinet Drawer Exploded View

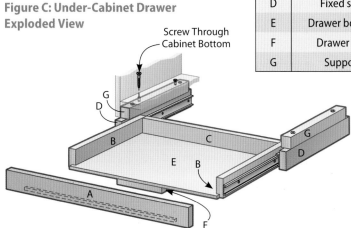

Screw Through Cabinet Bottom

EDITOR: TOM CASPAR • PHOTOGRAPHY: PHOTO AT LEFT BY AMY IRION, ALL OTHERS BY JOHN ENGLISH • ILLUSTRATION: FRANK ROHRBACH

by JOHN ENGLISH

Sycamore Pantry

THE BEST WAY TO MATCH SOLID WOOD AND VENEER IS TO MAKE THE VENEER YOURSELF

Sometimes you just fall in love with a special kind of wood. For me, that wood is quartersawn sycamore, but I've never had a chance to build something big that would really show it off. When my wife and I needed a new pantry for our kitchen, we found that commercial units were way too expensive, not very well crafted and used boring wood. I volunteered to make it myself. Out of sycamore, of course.

For ease of construction, I designed a pantry composed of four separate units. They're standard plywood boxes with face frames and overlay doors. The problem was, I didn't want to spend big bucks on custom-made quartersawn sycamore plywood. I considered buying some sycamore veneer and gluing it to a substrate myself, but then, I thought, it might not match the solid wood in the face frames.

My solution was to make my own thick veneer and design the boxes so I could mill all the parts on my 6-in. jointer, 14-in. bandsaw and 12-in. planer. It worked great, although I needed lots of clamps!

To build this pantry, you'll need about 60 bd. ft. of 4/4 quartersawn sycamore or a similar light-colored species, 10 bd. ft. of clear walnut, two sheets of 1/2-in. birch plywood and four sheets of 3/4-in. birch plywood. I prefer high-quality multi-ply plywood for casework. It has several more laminations than standard birch plywood, fewer voids, holds fasteners better and is generally more stable, flat and uniform.

Figure A: Exploded View

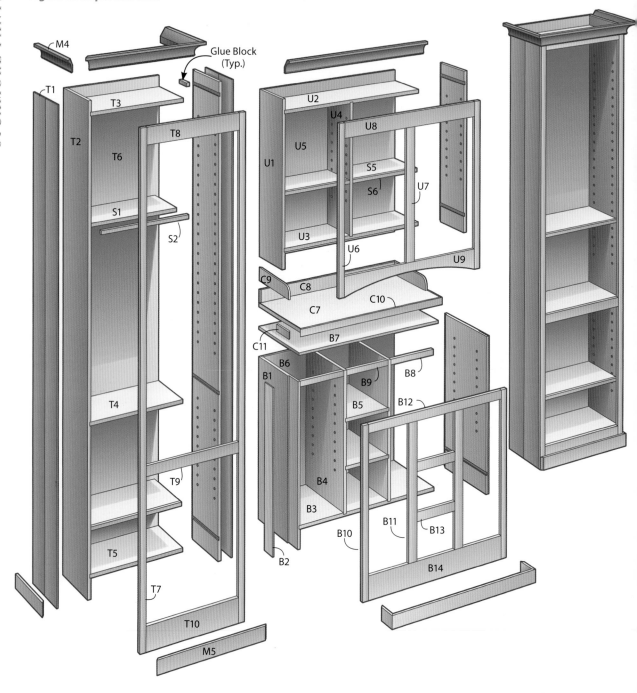

Glue Block (Typ.)

Figure B: Backside of Doors

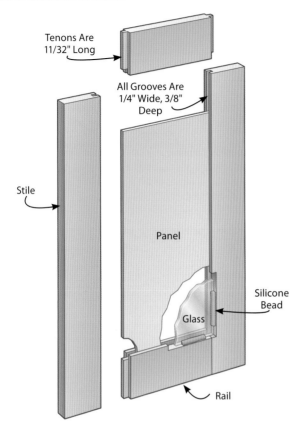

Tenons Are 11/32" Long

All Grooves Are 1/4" Wide, 3/8" Deep

Stile

Panel

Silicone Bead

Glass

Rail

This pantry really shows off the distinctive figure of quartersawn sycamore. To make thick veneer from sycamore boards, re-saw the best pieces down the middle.

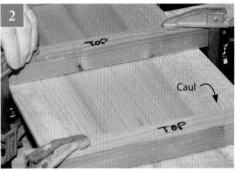

For the sides of the tall outer cabinets, glue the veneer to a plywood substrate, using curved cauls to distribute pressure. Run the panels through a planer to clean up the bandsawn surfaces.

Veneer the Side Units

1. Select seven 6-in. wide, 8-ft. long sycamore boards for re-sawing into veneer. Look for boards with the most interesting grain patterns. Plane the boards to 3/4 in. thick, then resaw them down the middle (Photo 1). Mark pieces from the same board so you can bookmatch them later.

2. Cut the side unit's plywood parts (T2 to T6).

3. Glue a pair of the veneers (T1) to the cabinet's sides (T2). You may have to joint these pieces first to make a tight seam. Use twelve pairs of cauls to glue each side (Photo 2).

4. Use a flush-trim router bit to even the veneer with the plywood's edges. Run the glue-up through a planer until the veneer is 3/16 in. thick, making the final side 7/8-in. thick (Photo 3). Trim the sides to final length.

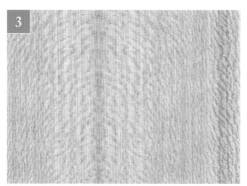

Here's one bookmatched panel, close up. When sycamore is quartersawn, you can clearly see its numerous ray cells scattered all over the surface. They give the wood an almost textured look.

Rabbet

The sides of the middle base cabinet are veneered, too, but not all the way across. Only a few inches of the sides project beyond the tall outer cabinets. Cut a wide rabbet to receive a 4-in. strip of veneer.

Veneer the Base Cabinet

5. Cut the plywood parts (B1 and B3 to B6). This cabinet projects only 3 in. beyond the tall cabinets, so there's no need to veneer the entire sides. You only need a 4 in. strip of veneer (B2, Fig. A). This veneer is let into a wide rabbet, which you can make on the tablesaw using a dado set (Photo 4). Clean up the rabbet with a block plane, if necessary.

6. Cut the veneer to size and plane it as thick as the rabbet is deep. Glue one piece to each side (Photo 5).

Glue the veneer onto the rabbet. This side is too wide to run through the planer after glue-up, so thickness-plane the veneer beforehand.

Join and Assemble

7. Cut the plywood parts for the upper unit (U1 to U4).

8. Rout dadoes and rabbets in all the cabinet's sides (Fig. C, D and E). Although the back for each cabinet is 1/2 in. thick, make its rabbets 5/8-in. wide. This allows for a 1/8-in. flange behind the back that can be scribed and trimmed later, so each cabinet can follow the contour of the wall when it is installed.

Space For Subtop

Pin-nail solid sycamore face frames to the cabinet sides. The center base unit's face frame extends above the cabinet's sides. This hides the front edge of a plywood subtop.

Figure C: Tall Cabinet Dadoes and Face Frame

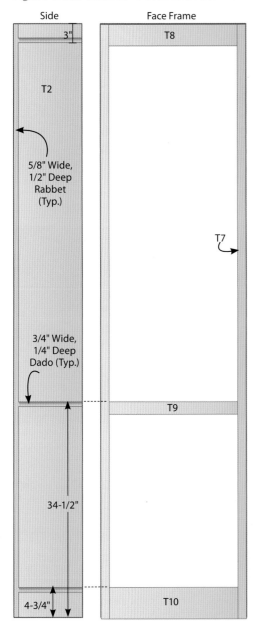

Side

Face Frame

3"

T2

T8

5/8" Wide, 1/2" Deep Rabbet (Typ.)

T7

3/4" Wide, 1/4" Deep Dado (Typ.)

T9

34-1/2"

4-3/4"

T10

Figure D: Base Cabinet Dadoes and Face Frame

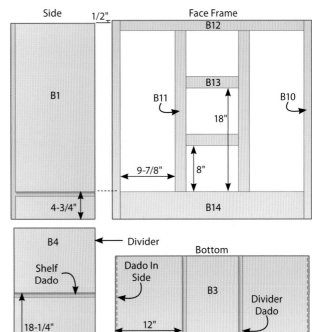

Side

1/2"

Face Frame

B12

B1

B13

B11

18"

B10

9-7/8"

8"

4-3/4"

B14

B4

Divider

Bottom

Shelf Dado

Dado In Side

B3

Divider Dado

18-1/4"

12"

1/4"

8-1/4"

Dado In Bottom

1/4"

Figure E: Upper Cabinet Dadoes and Face Frame

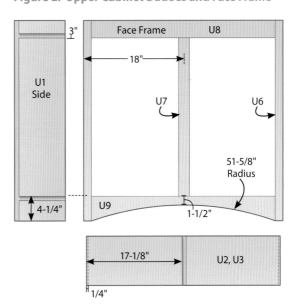

3"

Face Frame

U8

18"

U1 Side

U7

U6

51-5/8" Radius

4-1/4"

U9

1-1/2"

17-1/8"

U2, U3

1/4"

9. Glue and clamp the tops, fixed shelves and bottoms to the sides of all four cabinets. Drill holes for shelf supports before installing the backs, for easier access. For the upper unit, offset the holes in the divider (U4) by about 1/2 in. to the left or right or they will run into each other.

10. Install the backs with nails around the perimeter. Run screws into the top, fixed shelf and bottom. This strong joinery, combined with the back's substantial thickness, means that you won't have to install unsightly nailing strips to secure the cabinets to the wall.

Apply the Face Frames

11. Mill the face frame parts from the rest of your sycamore boards. Attach the rails to the stiles with biscuits, pocket screws or dowels.

The frames should be flush with the outside faces of the cabinets, and the top edge of both the bottom and fixed shelf need to line up with the top edge of the appropriate rails (Figs. C and D). Note that the face frame for the base cabinet is taller than the cabinet sides, to allow room for a subtop (B7).

12. Sand the face frames and clean out the corners with a chisel. Install the face frames with glue, finish nails and clamps (Photo 6). Fill the holes with birch-tinted putty.

13. Reinforce each cabinet's joints with many small glue blocks (Fig. A). Use more blocks behind the face frames, where they join the cabinets.

Build the door frames with extra-deep grooves so the solid-wood panels can expand in summer. Place soft-sponge Space Balls in the grooves to prevent the panels from rattling around in winter.

Build the glass doors in the upper cabinet the same way as the paneled doors. To make the glass easy to install from the back, turn the grooves into rabbets with a router.

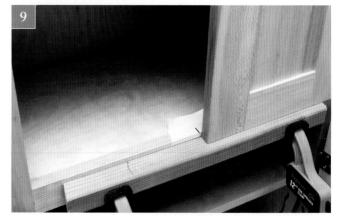

Hang the doors after the cabinets are installed, to make sure they're perfectly level. Support the doors on a ledger strip to line them up.

14. On the base unit, install cleats (B8 and B9) to support the subtop. Cut the subtop to size but don't attach it yet. It's a lot easier to install this cabinet without the subtop in place.

15. Make sycamore-edged shelves for all the cabinets. Trim the shelves 1/8-in. shorter than the distance between each cabinet's sides.

Make the Doors

16. Both the paneled and glass doors are constructed essentially the same way (Fig. B). Mill all the rails and stiles to size, then rout or dado a groove down the center of each part's inside edge.

17. Rout or dado tenons on the ends of each rail. Resaw bookmatched panels (T13, T16, and B17) from 3/4-in. thick boards and plane them to fit into the grooves. Apply finish to the panels before installing them.

18. Glue the doors together (Photo 7). Use Space Balls to prevent the panels from rattling in the winter when they shrink in width.

19. Rout a rabbet around the backside of the two glass doors using a bearing-guided rabbeting bit (Photo 8). Square the corners with a chisel. After applying a finish to the doors, install the glass. Use wooden retaining strips or a silicone bead to hold it in place.

Install the Cabinets

20. Sand all the components to 220 grit and apply a clear polyurethane finish.

21. Position the cabinets in your room. Determine the highest spot on your floor and place the cabinet that sits here first. Shim the remaining cabinets to align with this one. Attach the cabinets to the wall with screws driven through the backs and into your wall's studs.

22. Add pulls to the doors. Install the doors with full overlay hinges (Photo 9).

23. Make the crown molding (see Custom-Made Crown Molding, page 232), then fit it to the cabinets. Finish the molding as loose pieces, then pin-nail it to the cabinets, butted to the ceiling.

24. Add the base molding.

Make the Countertop

25. Glue the countertop (C7) from boards that are 4-in. or so wide, alternating heart and bark sides, to ensure that the top stays flat.

26. Install the subtop in the base unit. Trim the top to the exact width of the base unit. Screw and glue the countertop to the cleats (B8, B9). Install the backsplash (C8) and side pieces (C9). These hold the top down and allow for the top to expand and contract. Add the front and return trim (C10 and C11).

Figure F: Plywood Cutting Diagrams

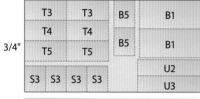

3/4"

3/4"

3/4"

3/4"

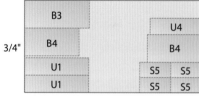

1/2"

1/2"

Cutting List				
Overall dimensions: 16-3/4"D x 84"W x 96"H				
Part	**Name**	**Qty.**	**Dimensions**	**Notes**
Tall Units				
Cabinets			11-1/4" D x 24" W x 95" H	
T1	Veneer	8	1/4" x 6" x 96"+	(A)
T2	Side	4	3/4" x 11-1/4" x 95"	(B)
T3	Top	2	3/4" x 10-5/8" x 22-3/4"	
T4	Fixed shelf	2	3/4" x 10-5/8" x 22-3/4"	
T5	Bottom	2	3/4" x 10-5/8" x 22-3/4"	
T6	Back	2	1/2" x 23" x 92-3/4"	
Face frames			24" W x 95" H	
T7	Stile	4	3/4" x 1-3/8" x 95"	
T8	Top rail	2	3/4" x 3-1/4" x 21-1/4"	
T9	Middle rail	2	3/4" x 2" x 21-1/4"	
T10	Bottom rail	2	3/4" x 4-3/4" x 21-1/4"	
Top doors			10-7/8" W x 58" H	
T11	Stile	8	3/4" x 2-3/4" x 58"	
T12	Rail	8	3/4" x 2-3/4" x 6"	
T13	Panel	4	1/4" x 6" x 53-1/8"	
Bottom doors			10-7/8" W x 28-1/2" H	
T14	Stile	8	3/4" x 2-3/4" x 28-1/2"	
T15	Rail	8	3/4" x 2-3/4" x 6"	
T16	Panel	4	1/4" x 6" x 23-5/8"	
Base Unit				
Cabinet			15" D x 36" W x 34-1/2" H	
B1	Side	2	3/4" x 15" x 34"	
B2	Veneer	2	1/4" x 4" x 34"	
B3	Bottom	1	3/4" x 14-1/2" x 35"	
B4	Divider	2	3/4" x 14-1/2" x 29-1/2"	
B5	Shelf	2	3/4" x 14-1/2" x 11-1/4"	
B6	Back	1	1/2" x 35" x 34"	
B7	Subtop	1	1/2" x 15" x 36"	
B8	Side cleat	2	3/4" x 1-1/4" x 11-1/4"	
B9	Middle cleat	1	3/4" x 1-1/4" x 10-3/4"	
Face frame			36" W x 34-3/4" H	
B10	Outer stile	2	3/4" x 1-3/8" x 34-1/2"	[C]
B11	Inner stile	2	3/4" x 2" x 28"	
B12	Top rail	1	3/4" x 1-3/4" x 33-1/4"	
B13	Middle rail	2	3/4" x 2" x 9-1/2"	
B14	Bottom rail	1	3/4" x 4-3/4" x 33-1/4"	
Doors			10-7/8" W x 28-1/2" H	
B15	Stile	4	3/4" x 2-3/4" x 28-1/2"	
B16	Rail	4	3/4" x 2-3/4" x 6"	
B17	Panel	2	1/4" x 6" x 23-5/8"	

Part	Name	Qty.	Dimensions	Notes
Upper Unit				
Cabinet			9" D x 36" W x 34-3/4" H	
U1	Side	2	3/4" x 9" x 34-3/4"	
U2	Top	1	3/4" x 8-1/2" x 35"	
U3	Bottom	1	3/4" x 8-1/2" x 35"	
U4	Divider	1	3/4" x 8-1/2" x 28"	
U5	Back	1	1/2" x 35" x 34-3/4"	
Face frame			36" W x 34-3/4" H	
U6	Outer stile	2	3/4" x 1-3/8" x 34-3/4"	
U7	Center stile	1	3/4" x 2" x 27-1/2"	
U8	Top rail	1	3/4"x 3" x 33-1/4"	
U9	Bottom rail	1	3/4" x 4-1/4" x 33-1/4"	
Doors			16-1/2" W x 28-1/2" H	
U10	Stile	4	3/4" x 2-3/4" x 28-1/2"	
U11	Rail	4	3/4" x 2-3/4" x 11-5/8"	
U12	Glass	2	Cut to fit	
Shelves				
S1	Tall unit	12	3/4" x 10" x 22-1/4"	
S2	Trim	12	3/8" x 3/4" x 22-1/4"	
S3	Base unit	4	3/4" x 13-5/8" x 11-1/4"	
S4	Trim	4	3/8" x 3/4" x 11-1/4"	
S5	Upper unit	4	3/4" x 7-7/8" x 16-7/8"	
S6	Trim	4	3/8" x 3/4" x 16-7/8"	
Countertop				
C7	Top	1	3/4" x 16-1/2" x 36"	
C8	Backsplash	1	3/8" x 2-3/4" x 36"	(D)
C9	Sides	2	3/8" x 2-3/4" x 11-5/8"	
C10	Front trim	1	1/4" x 1-1/4" x 36-3/4"	
C11	Return trim	2	1/4" x 1-1/4" x 4-7/8"	(E)
Molding				
M4	Crown	1	3/4" x 3" x 168"	(E)
M5	Base	1	1/2" x 2-3/4" x 120"	(D)
Hardware				
H1	Hinges	12 Pr.	Full overlay	
H2	Pulls	12	3" O/C	
H3	Shelf supports	80	1/4" diameter shaft	

by JOHN ENGLISH

Custom-Made Crown Molding

THIS EASY DETAIL ADDS A FINISHED LOOK

The biggest challenge in making your own crown molding is figuring out which cut to make when. Here's one solution. As you can see, it's all done on the tablesaw.

1. Make a cove (Cut 1) by running 24-in. or longer boards at 30 degrees to the blade. Guide the board in a jig and apply hold-down pressure with a pair of skateboard wheels. Start with a very shallow cut, then raise the blade in 1/16-in. increments until you've formed the full cove.

2. Tilt the blade 30 degrees for Cut 2. A handscrew prevents the molding from tipping. Use a zero-clearance insert plate if your plate doesn't provide adequate support.

3. Keeping the blade at 30 degrees, make Cut 3. The space between the blade and fence is very small. Cut a kerf through a piece of plywood to support the molding stock.

4. For Cut 4, leave the blade at 30 degrees. There should be enough room on your insert plate to support the molding this time.

5. With the blade still tilted at 30 degrees, make Cut 5.

6. Sand the molding with a large block. A can of beets (how fitting for a pantry!) is exactly the right size: just a little bit smaller in diameter than the cove.

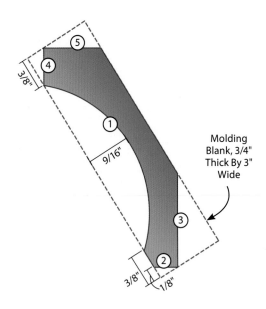

3/8"

9/16"

Molding Blank, 3/4" Thick By 3" Wide

3/8" 1/8"

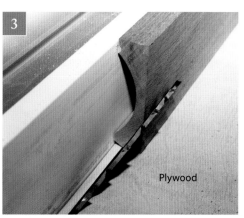

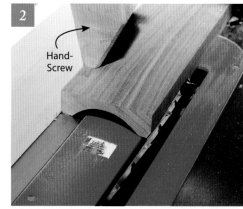

Hand-
Screw

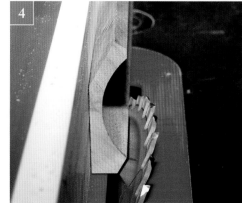

Plywood

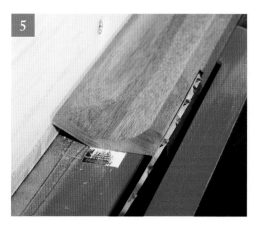

by RICK CHRISTOPHERSON

Appliance Garage

HIDE YOUR APPLIANCES BEHIND EXTRA-WIDE BI-FOLD DOORS

An appliance garage provides functional storage for the hodgepodge of appliances that clutter kitchen countertops. Close the doors, and everything is out of sight. Open the doors, and the appliances are at the ready.

Unlike most appliance garages that have a roll-top tambour door, this bifold door design provides twice the opening size, is easy enough to build in a weekend, and costs about $100. For smooth operation, a roller bearing and routed track guide the doors.

Most factory-built corner cabinets are 24-in. on each side with a 17-in. diagonal face. Measure yours to verify the size. If your cabinets are a different size from those in this story, you can resize the dimensions.

Figure A: Appliance Garage Exploded View

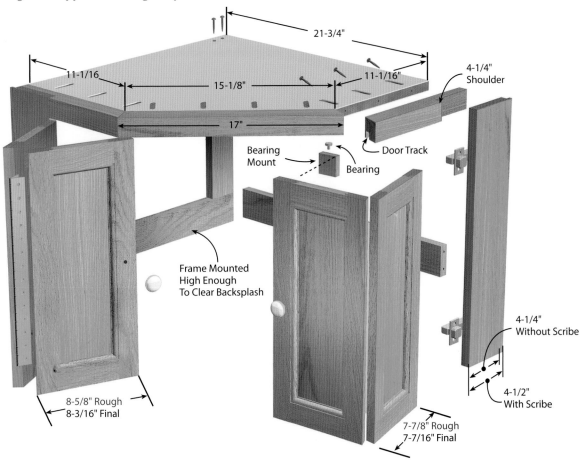

21-3/4"

11-1/16"

15-1/8"

11-1/16"

4-1/4"
Shoulder

17"

Door Track

Bearing
Mount

Bearing

Frame Mounted
High Enough
To Clear Backsplash

4-1/4"
Without Scribe

4-1/2"
With Scribe

8-5/8" Rough
8-3/16" Final

7-7/8" Rough
7-7/16" Final

Cutting the Top

To cut the top of the appliance garage, start out with a 21-3/4-in.-square piece of plywood or melamine-coated particle board. From this you need to cut the 45-degree face using the dimensions shown in Fig. A. If you don't have a sliding table on your tablesaw, you can use the miter-slot in your saw's table as a guide (Photo 1).

After the top is cut, drill for pocket holes across the front three edges, as shown in Photo 2. These pocket holes are used to secure the face frame.

Making the Face Frame

The face frame stock is 1-1/2-in. thick by 2-in. wide, and has 4-1/4-in. shoulders on each end where the frame meets the side stiles. The material is made from two pieces of 3/4-in. stock (48-in. by 2-1/8-in. by 3/4-in., and 39-in. by 2-1/8-in. by 3/4-in.) face-glued together. One piece is shorter than the other to create the shoulders. The stock is oversized to allow for trimming. Center the 39-in. piece onto the 48-in. piece and glue it so there is a 4-1/2-in. shoulder on each end. After the glue is dry, joint one edge so the pieces are flush. Rip and joint the other edge to 2-in.

Next, trim the ends of the board so the two shoulders are 4-1/4 in. long. With the miter saw set to 22-1/2 degrees, cut the face frame parts from this stock. I cut my joints slightly long at first to check the angles. When the joints are tight, I make the final cut to length without changing the saw's settings.

Installing the Face Frame

Using pocket-hole screws to secure the face frame to the top is the fastest and easiest method. After applying glue to the edges, clamp the right-hand frame to the plywood, and drive in the screws. The end of the frame should be flush with the back of the plywood. The top edges should be flush as well.

Next, attach the center part of the frame. Screw a clamping block to the top of the plywood, but make sure your screws don't poke all the way through the plywood top. With this in place, clamp the middle frame the same way you did the side frame (Photo 2). Finish with the left-hand frame piece.

Routing the Door Track

To rout the door track into the bottom edge of the face frame, you need a 9/16 in., top-bearing pattern bit for your plunge router. You'll also need to make a template for the router to follow.

Guide Strip

Caution! Saw guard removed for photo clarity. **Use yours!**

Cut the plywood top at 45 degrees using a 3⁄4-in. strip of scrap wood as a guide in your saw's miter slot. Screw the guide strip to the underside of the plywood.

Temporary Clamping Block

Install the face frame to the top using pocket-hole screws. The clamps hold the frame in place while the screws are driven in.

Resizing Your Garage

If your existing diagonal corner cabinet is not the same size as discussed in this story, you will have to modify the dimensions of the garage. The easiest method for changing the dimensions is to draw them out on a piece of plywood.

Draw the size of your existing corner cabinet on a sheet of plywood, then draw three offset lines at 3/4-in., 1-3/4-in., and 2-1/4-in. setback from the first. Because the appliance garage is 3/4-in. smaller than the existing cabinet, the 3/4-in. offset line is the front of the face frame and doors. To determine the size of the bifold doors, measure the length of the 3/4-in. offset line across the front and divide by two. This will be the width of the center doors. The outside doors are 3/4-in. narrower than the center doors. (Remember to make your doors 3/8-in. oversized for trimming.) Mark the width of the outside doors on the plywood. The width of the cabinet stiles can then be measured from this plywood template, but add an extra 1/4-in. to this measurement for the scribe.

The 1-3/4-in. offset line gives you the dimensions of the template for routing the door track, and the 2-1/4-in. offset line gives you the dimensions for the top of the cabinet.

Draw these layout lines to determine the dimensions of your appliance garage.

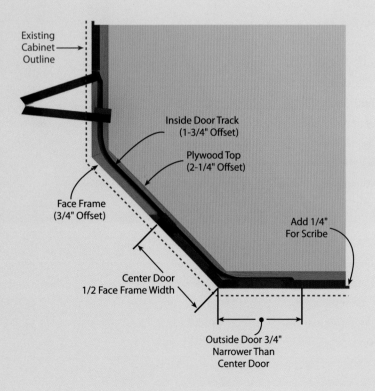

Existing Cabinet Outline

Inside Door Track (1-3/4" Offset)

Plywood Top (2-1/4" Offset)

Face Frame (3/4" Offset)

Add 1/4" For Scribe

Center Door 1/2 Face Frame Width

Outside Door 3/4" Narrower Than Center Door

Cut a piece of scrap plywood for the template which is 1-in. inset from the front of the face frame. Next, round the corners of the template with a 4-in. radius, using a smooth, sweeping motion with your belt sander.

Position the pattern 1 in. back from the front of the face frame, and clamp it down. Add spacers under the template for clamping.

Routing from left to right (counter-clockwise), make several shallow passes until the depth of the dado is about 1/2-in. (Photo 3). Don't let the router wander—jogs in the track will interfere with smooth door-roller operation. When completed, soften the sharp edges of the track and sand the inside of the dado.

Side Stiles and Frames

The vertical sides of the cabinet (the stiles) determine the height of the garage and support the doors. The length of the stiles should be 1/8-in. to 1/4-in. shorter than the distance from your countertop to the upper cabinet.

Rip the stiles to 4-1/2-in. wide (1/4-in. wider than the face frame shoulders), and cut them to the length needed. Then rabbet the back edge 1/4-in. wide by 1/2-in. deep to make scribing the cabinet to the wall easier.

When screwing the stiles to the face frame, angle the screws as shown in Photo 4 to draw the side joint tight. Because the doors attach to these stiles, it is very

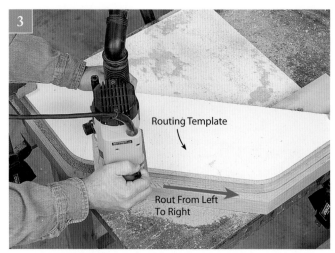

Rout the door track using a 9/16-in. pattern bit and template. Make several passes to reach the final depth of 1/2 in. The hold-down clamps also serve as guide stops for the stopped dado.

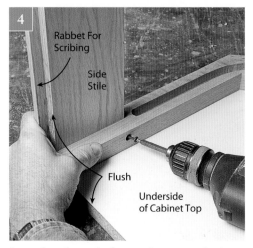

Screw the stiles to the frame using screws tilted at a slight angle to draw the side joint tight.

important that they are mounted square to the frame.

Using 2-in. frame stock, assemble the mounting frame (Fig. A) to the cabinet. Use pocket-hole construction to hold the frame together.

Building the Doors

This garage has a frame-and-panel door design to complement the existing doors. It takes two doors to make up each bifold. The outside doors are 7-7/8-in. wide, and the center doors are 8-5/8-in. wide. These dimensions are 3/8-in. oversized and will be trimmed off when the bevel is cut. The door height should be the same as the opening size. You'll trim the doors later when you square them.

After the doors are built, lightly sand them to flush-up the edges, but don't soften any of the corners yet. Joint one edge from each door. After measuring the cabinet to determine the size of each door, bevel-rip and joint the other edges at 22-1/2 degrees to fit the opening. After the doors are the proper width, square the tops and bottoms so each door is the same height.

Using a 1-3/8-in. Forstner bit, bore 1/2-in.-deep holes in the two outside doors for European cup hinges, positioned as shown in Fig. B. Then install the continuous (piano) hinge to the bifold pairs. To simplify the installation of the hinge, I taped the doors together tightly (Photo 5) before screwing the piano hinges in place.

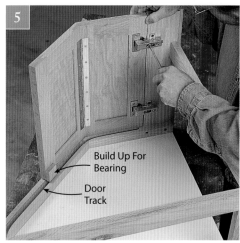

Install the hinge baseplates by attaching them to the hinges and fastening them to the stiles. Rough-adjust the hinges so the doors don't bind. Appliance garage turned upside down.

Figure B: Hinge Cup Location
Bore the hinge-cups in the door stiles at the position shown.

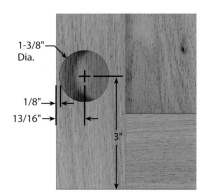

Next, plane a piece of 1-1/2-in.-wide stock to 1/2-in. thickness, and cut two pieces 1-1/2 in. by 1-1/2 in. by 1/2 in. Glue and clamp these pieces to the back side of the center doors (Fig. A). Make sure they are flush to the top and the outside edge where the bearings will be mounted.

Installing the Doors

I used European cup hinges for the doors because they have 3-dimensional adjustment capabilities. Cup hinges come in two parts—the hinge, and the baseplate. After predrilling the screw holes, screw the hinges to the doors. The baseplates have a small tab on the back that lines up with the edge of the face frame stiles. The easiest method for locating the baseplates is to attach them to the door hinges, place the door in position, and screw the baseplates to the cabinet (Photo 6).

With the doors mounted on the cabinet, locate the position of the track bearings. You have to determine the front-to-rear spacing to ensure the doors are flush to the face frame when closed and also the side-to-side placement so the doors don't bind when fully open. I found that a piece of clear packing tape made a good marking gauge. For the front-to-rear placement, I stuck the bearing to the back of the tape, and inserted it into the dado slot with the bearing touching the back wall of the dado. With a marker I traced the front corner of the face frame, as shown in Photo 7. To mark the side-to-side placement of the

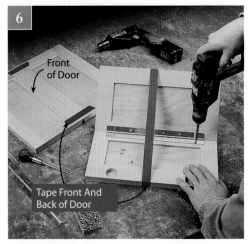

Install the piano hinge by taping the door joint closed.

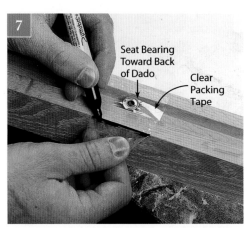

Mark the bearing locations using tape and a marker. Stick the bearing to the tape and locate it to the rear face of the dado. Mark the front edge of the face frame and transfer these locations to the door.

bearing, I placed the tape and bearing at the end of the track, fully opened the door, and marked where the edge of the door lined up with the tape.

Using the tape as a template, transfer these positions to the top corner of the door, and drill a hole for the bearing's screw. Because the forces on the bearing are side-to-side, you can mount it by just driving a No. 10 by 1-in. machine screw into the edge of the door.

Finishing the Garage

Sand the garage cabinet completely and soften any sharp edges. When you sand the doors, don't soften the miter joint corners unless the doors are closed. If you soften these corners separately, you will have a visible gap in the bifold. (If you use melamine, be careful not to scuff the surface—the wood stain will discolor it.)

To match the stain color with existing cabinets, take one of the original cabinet doors to a full-service paint store and have them custom-mix a stain to match.

Installing the Garage

The first step is to scribe the garage cabinet to fit the wall. I started by making a rough scribe to fit the existing back splash, as shown in Photo 8. This allowed the garage to be placed closer to the wall for a more accurate final scribe. The garage is 1/4-in. oversized, so remove as much of this as needed when fitting it to the wall.

Set Compass Width Equal To This Gap

Rough-scribe the cabinet to the existing back splash using a compass and a coping saw. After this is cut out, re-scribe the cabinet for final fit to the wall.

Locate the studs in the wall, and pilot-drill screw holes through the mounting frame. When you screw the cabinet to the wall, be careful not to rack the garage out of square; this will cause the doors to fit poorly. After the garage is in place, install molding to conceal the gap between the garage and the upper cabinet.

Finally, adjust the doors. There are three adjusting screws on each hinge. The front screw is used to flush the door with the face frame. The middle screw moves the door up and down, and the back screw adjusts the side-to-side placement of the door.

Now shove the toaster, the mixer, and the blender in the garage and shut the door. You've got counter space!

by SETH KELLER

Kitchen Stool

ROUND LEGS WITHOUT A LATHE

Few stools are as clean and elegant as this one. I built it with splayed legs to provide a stable footing. The multi-level rungs offer a variety of foot perches to satisfy just about anybody, no matter how short or tall they are. I topped it off with a gently scooped seat that's comfortable enough to permit lingering over a satisfying meal. I used contrasting wood for visual interest. I really like how the light-colored legs peek up through the dark seat. The legs and stretchers are made from strong, durable beech. The seat is made from cherry and reminds me of old, soft leather.

This project will keep your router humming and uses some very clever jigs to simplify and speed up construction. It's almost as easy to make half a dozen stools as it is to make one. Our stool is sized for a 36-in. counter height.

There will be a lot of parts floating around your shop as you build this stool and a lot of mortises to keep track of. So take my advice and mark your parts clearly as you go to avoid mix-ups.

Figure A: Exploded View

85 Deg.

Detail 1: Leg Mortise Layout

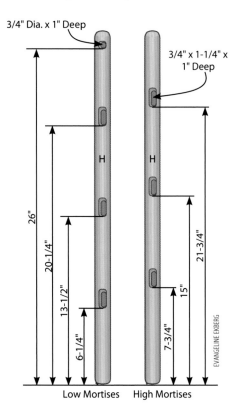

3/4" Dia. x 1" Deep

3/4" x 1-1/4" x 1" Deep

H

H

26"

20-1/4"

13-1/2"

6-1/4"

21-3/4"

15"

7-3/4"

EVANGELINE EKBERG

Low Mortises   High Mortises

Cutting List
Overall Dimensions: 28" x 16" x 16"

Part	Name	Qty.	Material	Dim. (Th x W x L)
A	Rung	2	Beech	3/4" x 1-1/4" x 14"
B	Rung	2	Beech	3/4" x 1-1/4" x 13-3/4"
C	Rung	2	Beech	3/4" x 1-1/4" x 12-3/4"
D	Rung	2	Beech	3/4" x 1-1/4" x 12-1/2"
E	Rung	2	Beech	3/4" x 1-1/4" x 11-9/16"
F	Rung	2	Beech	3/4" x 1-1/4" x 11-5/16"
G	Stretcher	2	Beech	3/4" x 1-1/4" x 10-5/8"
H	Leg	4	Beech	1-7/16" x 1-7/16" x 28"
J	Seat	1	Cherry	1-1/4" x 13" x 13"

PROJECT REQUIREMENTS AT A GLANCE

Special Tools:
- Plunge Router

Lumber Quantity:
- 4 bf. 8/4 Beech, 4 bf. 4/4

Mortise the Legs

1. Mill the leg blanks (H) and cut them to length.

2. Lay out the mortises (Fig. A, above) (Photo 1). The mortises are offset so one set of rungs (B, D, and F) are positioned higher on the leg than the other set (A, C, E, and G). Mark the higher mortises first, then rotate the legs and mark the lower ones (Photo 2).

3. Rout the mortises using a jig and a 3/4-in. plunge router bit (Fig. B, page 246) (Photo 3). Orient each leg in the jig in the same manner: the top of each leg should stick out of the jig's indexed end. Make the round seat stretcher mortise with a single plunge.

4. Roundover the edges of the legs with a 3/4-in. roundover bit (Photo 4.) Round over the ends of each leg with a 3/8-in. roundover bit (Photo 5.)

Rungs and Stretchers

5. Round over four 5-foot long pieces of rung stock with a 3/8-in. roundover (Photo 6). The ends of each stretcher fit like tenons into the leg mortises. As you mill the rungs, use some extra stock to

Begin building the stool by laying out mortises on the legs. The mortises are offset with one set higher than the other. Clamp the legs together and lay out all the high mortises first. I like to shade each mortise to avoid mistakes.

Cut the angled mortises with a jig and a plunge router. To position the leg, line up the top of the mortise with the top of the index notch on the jig.

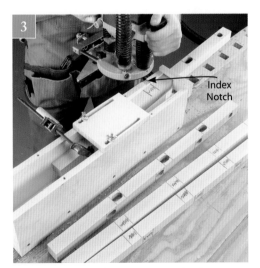

To layout the lower mortises, rotate the two outside legs 90 degrees away from the center. Then roll the two center legs away from the center as well. This automatically positions the correct face of each leg.

Round over all four corners on the legs. When you're done, they'll almost look like they were turned. A featherboard maintains consistent pressure against the fence.

Figure B: Mortising Jig

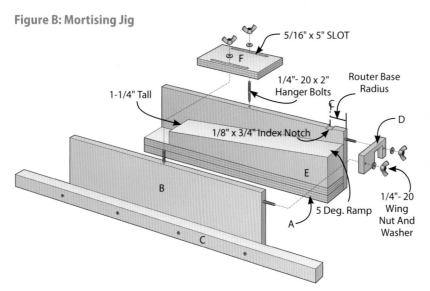

5/16" x 5" SLOT

F

1/4"- 20 x 2"
Hanger Bolts

Router Base
Radius

1-1/4" Tall

1/8" x 3/4" Index Notch

C

D

With the end stop in place (D), rout an index notch on the jig to ensure proper alignment of the leg in the jig.

E

B

5 Deg. Ramp

A

1/4"- 20 Wing Nut And Washer

C

test and fine-tune your cuts by adjusting the bit height or fence position. You should be able to insert the rungs into the mortises by hand.

6. Cut the rungs and seat stretchers to length and label them. Shape the seat stretchers on the bandsaw (Photo 7).

7. Create the 3/4-in. round tenons on the seat stretchers (Photo 8). Drill pilot holes for the screws that attach the seat (Fig. A).

Assemble the Base

8. Dry fit all of the base parts.

9. Glue up the base in stages (Photo 9). Place a straightedge on the seat stretchers to make sure they lay flat to support the seat (Photo 10.) Be sure to measure the top diagonally for square.

Cutting List: Mortising Jig			
Part	Name	Qty.	Dim. (Th x W x L)
A	Bottom	2	3/4" x 3-1/4" x 24"
B	Side	2	3/4" x 6" x 24"
C	Clamp Rail	1	1" x 1-1/2" x 30"
D	End Stop*	1	3/4" x 1-3/4" x 4-3/4"*
E	Ramp**	1	3" x 3-1/4 x 18
F	Adj. Stop	1	3/4 x 4-3/4 x 6"

* Cut the notch to accommodate leg stock.
** Ramp tapers from 3" to 1-1/4"

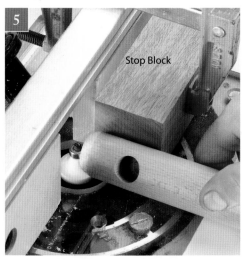

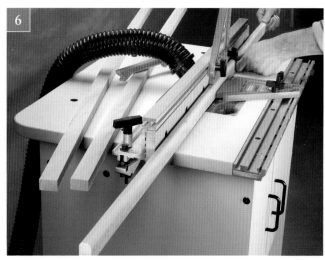

Round over the ends of each leg. Hold the leg tight against a stop block as you feed it into the bit. When the leg contacts the bearing, rotate it slowly to complete the roundover.

Mill roundovers on long lengths of rung stock. Cut the rungs and seat stretchers to length afterward. This is more efficient and safer than shaping short lengths. Featherboards produce a clean, consistent cut.

Shape the seat stretchers on the bandsaw. It's best to make two cuts. Cut the short angle first, then make the long straight cut.

Cut the round tenons on the seat stretchers. When the cut hits the wide part of the stretcher, let it ride on the bearing until it contacts the fence on the outfeed side.

Make the Seat

10. Glue up a cherry blank. When the glue is dry, trim the blank to 13" square.

11. Draw diagonal lines from each corner on the underside of the seat and drill a 1/4-in. hole in the center for the index pin in the seat-scooping jig (Fig. D, page 251).

12. Lay out the top of the seat blank (Fig. C).

13. Drill the leg holes in the seat blank (Photo 11).

14. Cut the seat to shape on the bandsaw: sand it smooth.

15. Place the seat blank in the seat-scooping jig (Fig. D, page 251) and screw the rails into place so they put firm pressure on the seat.

16. Scoop out the seat using a long straight bit (Photo 12).

17. Round over the edges of the seat around the leg holes with a 3/8-in. roundover bit. Use a 3/4-in. roundover bit on the outside edges of the seat.

18. Sand the entire stool to 180-grit if you'll be finishing the stool with varnish or lacquer. Use 220-grit if you plan on an oil or a wipe-on varnish finish.

19. Attach the seat to the base (Photo 13).

Stretcher

Glue up the base in sections. Have all of your parts labeled and laid out in sequence. Glue up the two halves with the three mortises first. When they're dry, glue up the whole stool together with the seat stretcher and remaining rungs.

Figure C: Seat Blank Layout

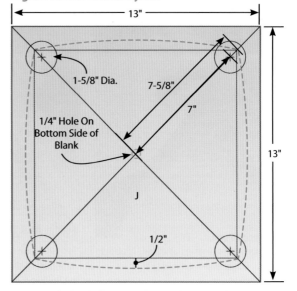

13"

1-5/8" Dia.

7-5/8"

7"

1/4" Hole On Bottom Side of Blank

13"

J

1/2"

To layout the leg holes, draw diagonal lines on the seat blank and measure 7" from the center out to each corner. This marks the center of each hole. Measure 7-5/8" to mark the four corners of the finished seat. Use a flexible stick to mark the 1/2" bow on the four edges.

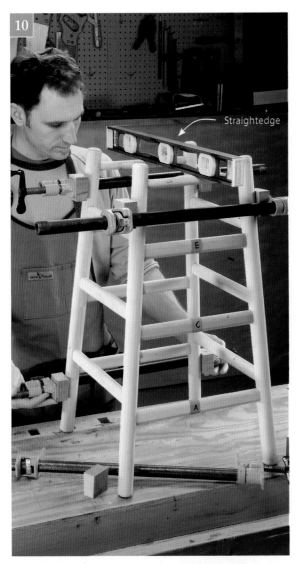

Clamp up the base on a flat surface. Angled blocks will prevent the clamps from slipping. Use a straightedge to make sure the wide section on the seat stretchers lies flat.

Bore leg holes through the seat blank. Clamp the blank to a sacrificial table to prevent blowout. Cut the curved sides on the bandsaw after drilling the holes.

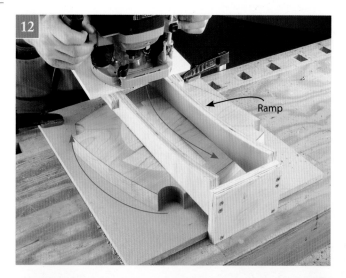

Scoop the seat with a router and a simple jig. Slide your router across the curved ramp. Rotate the seat a router bit's worth after each pass. Keep the cuts shallow.

It's best to pre-finish the seat and base before final assembly. Then simply attach the seat to the stretchers with screws.

Figure D: Scooping Jig

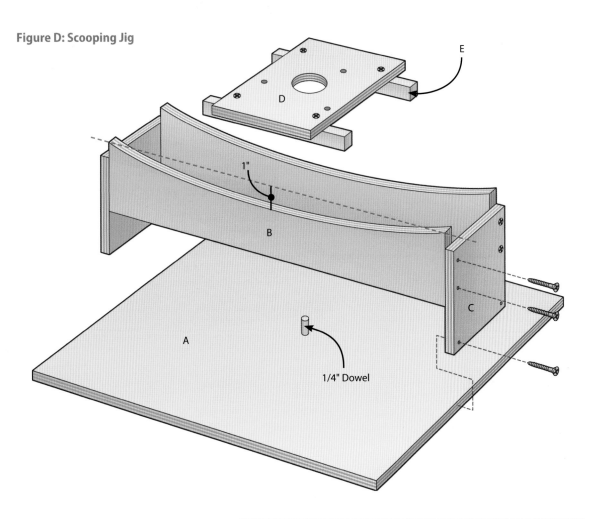

E

D

1"

B

C

A

1/4" Dowel

Cutting List: Scooping Jig

Part	Name	Qty.	Material	Dim. Th x W x L
A	Base	1	Plywood	3/4" x 18" x 18"
B	Ramp	2	Plywood	3/4" x 2-5/8" x 18"
C	End	2	Plywood	3/4" x 3-3/4" x 5-1/8"
D	Sub-base	1	Plywood	1/2" x 6" x 8"
E	Runners	2	Plywood	3/4" x 1" x 8"

Index

Index

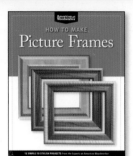
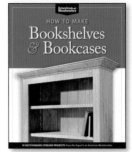
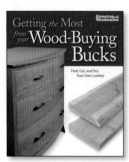
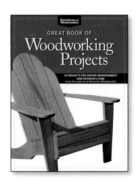

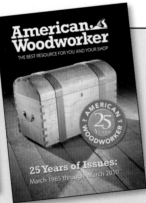